ARCO

MAT
MILLER ANALOGIES TEST

William Bader
M.S. English/Education
P.D. Supervision/Administration
and
Daniel S. Burt, Ph.D.

ARCO PUBLISHING, INC.
NEW YORK

First Edition, Second Printing, 1983

Published by Arco Publishing, Inc.
219 Park Avenue South, New York, N.Y. 10003

Library of Congress Cataloging in Publication Data

Bader, William.
    Miller analogies test.

    Third ed. by: Edward C. Gruber. 1972.
    1. Miller analogies test.   I. Burt, Daniel S.
II. Gruber, Edward C. Miller analogies test.
III. Title.
LB2367.6.B32 (P+P) 1981   371.2'62   81-152
ISBN 0-668-04989-8 (Library Edition)   AACR2
ISBN 0-668-04990-1 (Paper Edition)

Printed in the United States of America

CONTENTS

PART THREE: VERBAL ANALOGIES FOR COLLEGE ENTRANCE AND OTHER GRADUATE-LEVEL EXAMINATIONS

THE MILLER ANALOGIES TEST

WHAT IS THE MAT?

The Miller Analogies Test, commonly referred to as the MAT, is a high level test of mental ability required by many graduate schools for admission to a master's or doctoral program or as a basis for granting financial aid for graduate study. The test is also required by some business firms and some scientific, social and educational agencies for employment in jobs calling for a high degree of intellectual ability.

The MAT is administered by the Psychological Corporation at hundreds of test centers located throughout the United States, Canada, Australia, Great Britain and the Philippines. A complete list of testing centers together with specific information about applying for and taking the MAT is included in the official bulletin of information for the MAT, available upon request from The Psychological Corporation, 304 East 45th Street, New York, New York 10017.

THE NATURE OF THE TEST

The MAT consists of 100 analogies—mostly verbal—which are to be answered in only 50 minutes. The questions cover a broad range of subjects with only a smattering of items in any one field of study. Although considered an aptitude test, the MAT presupposes not only an extensive vocabulary but also a firm grounding in literature, social studies, mathematics and science.

In general, MAT questions are arranged in order of difficulty with the easiest questions at the beginning of the test. However, all questions are of equal weight and no penalty is imposed for incorrect responses. Therefore, it is to your advantage to proceed through the test as quickly as possible, answering every question you can. When you have done this, go back and answer the questions you skipped, even if you have to guess.

HOW SCORES ARE REPORTED

Within a few days after taking the MAT, you will receive a report of your score on a card which you addressed to yourself at the time of the test. This card is for your personal records only.

At about the same time, official reports of your test score will be sent to those institutions, agencies or companies you designated at examination time. You are entitled to as many as three official score reports provided that you specify complete, correct addresses for each one on the day you take the test. After the test date, you will have to pay an additional fee for any further reports of your test score that you may wish to have sent out.

Only raw scores are reported by the Psychological Corporation. It is left to the receiving institution to interpret these scores according to their own standards or norms as established through past experience with MAT scores.

WHAT ABOUT RETESTING?

It is *recommended* that you retake the MAT if you are required to submit your score more than two years after taking the test. It is *necessary* to retake the test if scores are required more than five years after the initial test. If you choose to retake the test in a period of less than 24 months, both current and previous scores are reported. If you retake the test within a 12-month period, you must request an alternate form for the second examination; otherwise the results will be invalidated.

Part I
Preparing for the MAT

ALL ABOUT ANALOGIES

WHAT IS AN ANALOGY?

An analogy is a verbal proportion presented in the following form:

$$A : B :: C : D$$

In this proportion the sign : stands for *is to* and the sign :: stands for *as*. Therefore, the problem above is read A is to B as C is to D.

On the MAT one of the four terms in each analogy is missing. The missing term may be in the first, second, third or fourth position in the proportion. In place of the missing term are four options enclosed in parentheses and lettered a, b, c and d. The task is to choose the one option which best completes the analogy: that is, the option which establishes the same relationship between the terms of the incomplete word pair as you have determined exists between the terms of the given word pair.

SEEKING A RELATIONSHIP BETWEEN THE GIVEN TERMS

The first step in solving an analogy problem is to find a relationship between two of the three given terms. In MAT analogies the relationship may be between the two terms on the left side of the proportion and the two terms on the right side of the proportion such that A is related to B as C is related to D. Or the relationship may cross the proportion sign so that A is related to C as B is related to D. Never give up on an analogy problem until you have considered both of these possibilities. A look at the following sample questions will illustrate this point.

1. DOCTOR : SYMPTOM :: DETECTIVE : (a. mystery, b. crime, c. police, d. clue)
2. DOCTOR : DETECTIVE :: SYMPTOM : (a. illness, b. mystery, c. crime, d. clue)

In the first sample question it is fairly obvious that a relationship exists between the first two terms (a and b): to the DOCTOR a SYMPTOM provides the key to the nature of an illness. The same relationship may be established between the third and fourth terms (c and d): to the DETECTIVE a CLUE provides the key to the nature of a crime.

In the second sample question no relationship is immediately apparent between the first two terms. However, when you consider the first and third terms (a and c) and the second and fourth terms (b and d), the relationship of an investigator to a piece of evidence should come to light.

Bear in mind that it is never acceptable to relate the first and fourth terms (a and d) to the second and third terms (b and c).

Whether an analogy is in the form of A : B :: C : D or A : C :: B : D, the direction of the relationship must be the same on both sides of the analogy. In other words, if the relationship between the terms of the given word pair is that the first term is part of the second term, then the relationship of the incomplete word pair must also be that the first term is part of the second. Sample question 3 illustrates this point.

3. MINUTE : HOUR :: MONTH : (a. week, b. year, c. time, d. calendar)

The relationship established by terms A and B is one of part to whole; a MINUTE is part of an HOUR. In order to maintain the same relationship, the second word pair must also be part to whole; a MONTH is part of a YEAR. If you select week, you are reversing the direction of the relationship required by the given word pair and thus making an unacceptable analogy.

CLASSIFYING ANALOGIES

There are two techniques that may be employed to determine the nature of the relationship between the terms in a verbal analogy—one using sentences and one using categories. In the Sentence Technique you begin by making up a short, simple sentence using the two terms you are considering. Then you substitute the other given term, together with each of the answer choices, in the sentence you have created. You should find one combination that exactly parallels the relationship expressed by the original word pair. An analysis of the following sample question illustrates the Sentence Technique for solving analogy problems.

PLAY : AUDIENCE :: BOOK : (a. writer, b. publisher, c. plot, d. reader)

Step 1. Make a short sentence using the first two terms:
A *play* is meant to entertain an *audience*.
Step 2. Substitute the third term and each of the answer choices in the same sentence:
a. A *book* is meant to entertain a *writer*.
(It certainly may, but this is hardly the purpose of a book.)
b. A *book* is meant to entertain a *publisher*.
(Again, a book that entertains publishers only has a very limited appeal.)
c. A *book* is meant to entertain a *plot*.
(This statement can be eliminated immediately since it makes no sense.)
d. A *book* is meant to entertain a *reader*.
(This statement is both parallel to the original statement and true; therefore, it is correct.)
The Category Technique for classifying analogies involves devising a list of

common relationships between words. This list must be comprehensive enough to describe almost every way in which words can be related and yet concise enough to be committed to memory. Through careful analysis of thousands of analogy questions, we were able to distinguish eighteen categories into which the vast majority of analogies fall. These categories are intended to serve as *guidelines* for analogical thinking. They are by no means the only relationships that can exist among terms, nor are they mutually exclusive. A single analogy problem may fit into two—or even three—different categories, as for example, PAINTING : WALL :: RUG : FLOOR. Whether you consider this an analogy of association or place or even purpose, you can still select the correct term to complete the relationship.

The following list of common relationships represents our exhaustive analysis of the analogy question. Study it well, for it will prove invaluable to you as you work your way through the practice tests in this book and, more importantly, as you take the actual MAT.

1. *SYNONYMS OR SIMILAR CONCEPTS*
   DELIVERANCE : (a. rescue, b. oration, c. liberate, d. demise) : : EXERCISE : PRACTICE
   The given terms in this analogy consist of a noun and two verbs. The verbs, EXERCISE and PRACTICE, are synonyms. Therefore, the missing term must be a noun, which means the same as DELIVERANCE, in this case, RESCUE.

2. *ANTONYMS OR CONTRASTING CONCEPTS*
   (a. hostel, b. hostile, c. amenable, d. amoral) : AMICABLE :: CHASTE : LEWD
   The relationship existing between CHASTE (meaning pure or decent) and LEWD) meaning obscene or salacious) is that they are opposites. The opposite of AMICABLE is HOSTILE.

3. *CAUSE AND EFFECT*
   HEREDITY : ENVIRONMENT :: (a. influenza, b. pneumonia, c. hemophilia, d. roseola) : RUBELLA
   In this analogy, the cause-and-effect relationship is easier to see when you consider the second and fourth terms as the given word pair. A virus present in the ENVIRONMENT is the cause of RUBELLA (German measles). Similarly, a sex-linked gene which is part of one's HEREDITY is the cause of HEMOPHILIA (a blood defect characterized by delayed clotting of the blood).

4. *PART TO WHOLE*
   LEAF : TREE :: KEY : (a. lock, b. door, c. typewriter, d. car)
   The relationship between the first two terms is that a LEAF is one small part of the whole TREE. A KEY is used to open a lock or a door or a car, but the only term to which key can be related as one small part of a whole is TYPEWRITER.

5. *PART TO PART*
   FATHER : DAUGHTER :: GILL : (a. fish, b. fin, c. lung, d. wattle)
   FATHER and DAUGHTER are each part of a family. GILL and FIN are each part of a fish. If you pair gill with fish, you are changing the part-to-part relationship required by the first pair of terms to a part-to-whole relationship and thus making an unacceptable analogy.

6. *PURPOSE OR USE*
   GLOVE : BALL :: HOOK : (a. coat, b. line, c. fish, d. curve)
   A GLOVE is used to catch a BALL just as a HOOK is used to catch a FISH. A hook may also be used to hold a coat, but this relationship is not as close to the relationship expressed by the given word pair as is hook and fish.

7. *ACTION TO OBJECT*
   PITCH : FIRE :: (a. coal, b. ball, c. sound, d. slope) : GUN
   You might be tempted to look for a synonym relationship in this analogy since pitch and fire both mean to hurl with force. However, since none of the answer choices is a synonym for gun this relationship must be ruled out. On re-examination look for a relationship between the second and fourth terms. This should lead to the realization that to FIRE is an action taken on a GUN just as to PITCH is an action taken on a BALL.

8. *OBJECT TO ACTION*
   SPRAIN : (a. ankle, b. tape, c. twist, d. swell) :: BITE : ITCH
   The problem in this analogy is to determine whether the given terms are being used as nouns or verbs. Once you realize that sprain and bite are used as nouns and itch is used as a verb, you can see the relationship of an object to the action taken upon it. Recognizing this relationship, you can then pinpoint the verb swell as the correct answer, for just as a BITE is likely to ITCH, a SPRAIN is likely to SWELL.

9. *PLACE*
   PARAGUAY : BOLIVA :: SWITZERLAND : (a. Afghanistan, b. Germany, c. Czechoslovakia, d. Yugoslavia)
   Paraguay, Boliva and Switzerland are all landlocked countries. So, too, are Afghanistan and Czechoslovakia. In order to complete this analogy the relationship among the given terms must be further refined. PARAGUAY and BOLIVA are landlocked countries in South America. SWITZERLAND and CZECHOSLOVAKIA are landlocked countries in Europe. (Afghanistan is in Asia.)

10. *ASSOCIATION*
    MOZART : MUSIC :: PEI : (a. painting, b. architecture, c. sculpture, d. dance)
    MOZART, the eighteenth-century Austrian composer, is associated with the field of MUSIC in the same way that PEI, the twentieth-century Chinese-American architect is associated with the field of ARCHITECTURE.

11. *SEQUENCE OR TIME*

    SAIL : STEAM :: PROPELLER : (a. plane, b. engine, c. jet, d. wing)
    Ships were propelled first by SAIL and later by STEAM. Similarly, planes
    were propelled first by means of a PROPELLER and later by means of a
    JET engine.

12. *CHARACTERISTIC OR DESCRIPTION*

    (a. scream, b. ear, c. shrill, d. vocal) : PIERCING :: CRY : PLAINTIVE
    A CRY may be described as PLAINTIVE, meaning woeful, just as a
    SCREAM may be described as PIERCING, meaning loud and shrill. If
    you have trouble with an analogy such as this in which the missing term is
    the first term in the question, try reversing the first and second terms.
    Remember, though, that if you reverse the first pair of terms, you must
    also reverse the second pair in order to preserve the original relationship.
    In this example, you may find it easier to choose the correct answer when
    the adjectives piercing and plaintive are placed in the more usual position
    of coming before, rather than after, the nouns they modify.

13. *DEGREE*

    WARM : HOT :: BRIGHT : (a. dark, b. dim, c. genius, d. illuminate)
    WARM is a lesser degree of temperature than HOT. BRIGHT is a lesser
    degree of intelligence than GENIUS. Remember that the direction of the
    relationship must be the same on each side of the analogy. Since the
    progression from warm to hot is an increase in degree, you must choose an
    answer that represents an increase in degree over the given term bright.

14. *MEASUREMENT*

    ODOMETER : (a. speed, b. distance, c. pressure, d. temperature) ::
    CLOCK : TIME
    A CLOCK measures TIME passed just as an ODOMETER measures
    DISTANCE traveled.

15. *GRAMMATICAL*

    BROKE : BROKEN :: (a. fled, b. flight, c. flew, d. flung) : FLOWN
    BROKE and BROKEN are respectively the past tense and past participle
    of the verb break. FLEW and FLOWN are the past tense and past
    participle of the verb fly. In addition to tenses of verbs, grammatical
    analogies may be concerned with parts of speech and formation of plurals.

16. *MATHEMATICAL*

    12 1/2% : (a. 1/4, b. 1/5, c. 1/8, d. 1/3) :: 16 2/3% : 1/6
    This problem illustrates one kind of mathematical analogy—an equality.
    Since percents are fractions whose denominators are always 100, 12 1/2%
    equals 12 1/2 divided by 100, which equals 1/8. Similarly, 16 2/3% equals
    16 2/3 divided by 100, which equals 1/6. Other common mathematical
    analogies concern geometrical and numerical relationships.

17. *WORKER TO TOOL*
   PHYSICIAN : (a. hospital, b. patient, c. surgeon, d. X-ray) :: ACTUARY
   : STATISTICS
   An ACTUARY uses STATISTICS as a tool in calculating insurance and
   annuity premiums. A PHYSICIAN uses an X-RAY as a tool in
   diagnosing and treating a patient.

18. *NON-SEMANTIC*
   HOE : ROE :: THOUGH : (a. rough, b. flood, c. flow, d. how)
   In this sample question the terms are related not by meaning but by sound.
   The only relationship among the three given terms is the fact that they
   rhyme. Of the answer choices, only FLOW rhymes with HOE, ROW and
   THOUGH.

   EVIL : LIVE :: STEP : (a. stand, b. stop, c. post, d. pest)
   Another common non-semantic relationship concerns the arrangement of
   letters in a word. In this sample question EVIL and LIVE are two words
   made up of the same letters in different arrangements. An alternate
   arrangement of the letters in STEP results in the word PEST.

ANALOGY TEST-TAKING TIPS

1. Read each question carefully and try to categorize the relationship
   expressed by the given word pair. First look for a relationship between the
   two given words separated by a single colon (A and B or C and D). If you
   find no relationship between these terms, then look for a relationship
   between the first and third or the second and fourth terms (A and C or B
   and D).
2. Read each answer choice. It has been shown that the questions most likely
   to be answered incorrectly are those in which the correct answer is the last
   option. The most probable reason for this is that candidates tend to choose
   the first plausible answer they see, rather than examining all four options
   to determine which is truly the best answer to the question.
3. Use context clues to solve analogy problems containing one or more
   unfamiliar terms. While all four terms in an analogy question need not be
   the same part of speech, there will be no more than two parts of speech
   represented in any one question (unless the question is a non-semantic
   analogy). With this fact in mind, you can immediately eliminate any
   option which introduces a third part of speech into an analogy problem.
4. Answer every question. MAT scores are based solely on the number of
   questions you answer correctly. Since there is no penalty imposed for
   incorrect responses, it is to your advantage to mark an answer for every
   question. Even if you are only guessing, you just might hit the right answer
   and add valuable points to your score. You lose nothing if you are wrong.
5. Work quickly. You have only fifty minutes to answer one hundred analogy
   problems. That means you should allow fewer than thirty seconds per
   question. Don't waste time stewing over a difficult analogy. If the answer

does not come easily, go on to the next question and answer every question you know—or even think you know—in the entire exam. Save five minutes at the end of the test to go back and answer the questions you skipped. If you still have no idea which answer is correct, then guess.

6. Come to the examination supplied with a watch and two or three pencils with erasers. Because it is so important for you to pace yourself on the MAT, it is essential that you be aware of the time. It is faster and easier to glance at your own watch than to look around the room for a clock to track your progress. Obviously, you do not want to waste precious time sharpening pencils or searching for an eraser to change an answer.

7. Become familiar with MAT question types by working through each of the practice tests and sample exams in this book. While the test you take may not have any of the same questions as the practice tests, it will certainly cover many of the same relationships between terms. As you sharpen your ability to recognize these relationships, you will be increasing your chances of scoring high on the MAT.

ANALOGY TESTS CLASSIFIED BY CATEGORY

Start your preparation for the MAT by taking each of the tests that follow. These tests provide intensive practice with the Category Technique for solving analogy problems. Each test consists of twenty-six questions which are indicative of the range of possibilities within a given category. The thirteen-minute time limit for each test simulates the pace of the MAT, a pace that requires quick decisions and allows for no dawdling over elusive relationships.

When you have completed these tests, check your answers with the correct answers at the end of the chapter. If you are not satisfied with your performance on the practice tests, try them again. If your scores show that you have a good grasp of the analogy question, move on to tackle the five full-length sample exams that follow.

The sample exams contain a mixture of analogy problems very much like the mixture on the actual MAT. In addition to correct answers, explanations are provided after each exam to show you where and how you may have gone astray in answering each question. Take time to read these explanations for they may help to keep you from making some of the more common errors on your exam.

VERBAL ANALOGIES TEST I. SYNONYMS
Time: 13 minutes. 26 Questions.

Directions: Each of these test questions consists of three CAPITALIZED words and four lettered words enclosed in parentheses. Two of the capitalized words are related in some way. Find the two related words lettered a, b, c and d. Select the one lettered word which is related to the remaining capitalized word in the same way that the first two capitalized words are related. Mark the Answer Sheet for the letter preceding the word you select. Answer Sheets for all tests in this section begin on page 151.

1. DILIGENT : UNREMITTING :: DIAMETRIC : (a. pretentious, b. geographical, c. adamant, d. opposite)

2. REMUNERATIVE: PROFITABLE :: FRAUDULENT : (a. deceit, b. slander, c. fallacious, d. plausible)

3. EXTORT : WREST :: CONSPIRE : (a. entice, b. plot, c. deduce, d. respire)

4. WIDOW : DOWAGER :: CONSORT : (a. enemy, b. constable, c. companion, d. distaff)

5. GAUDY : OSTENTATIOUS :: DEJECTED : (a. oppressed, b. inform, c. rejected, d. depressed)

6. BASS : LOW :: SOPRANO : (a. intermediate, b. feminine, c. alto, d. high)

7. ELEGANCE : LUXURY :: POVERTY : (a. penury, b. misery, c. poorhouse, d. hunger)

8. ARTIFICE : FINESSE :: INEPT : (a. inefficient, b. artistic, c. tricky, d. insatiable)

9. REGISTER : ENROLL :: REGALE : (a. endure, b. remain, c. feast, d. cohere)

10. ESTABLISH : BEGIN :: ABOLISH : (a. slavery, b. wrong, c. abolition, d. end)

11. STREW : DISPERSE :: STRAY : (a. deviate, b. utter, c. dredge, d. relegate)

12. PROSTRATE : FLAT :: VERTICAL : (a. circular, b. plumb, c. horizontal, d. inclined)

13. DISTANT : REMOTE :: NATIVE : (a. indigenous, b. Indian, c. foreign, d. godly)

14. BLAST : GUST :: BLARE : (a. uncover, b. roar, c. blaze, d. icicle)

15. DIURNAL : DAILY :: NOCTURNAL : (a. evening, b. seasonal, c. equinoctial, d. nightly)

16. INCIPIENT : BEGINNING :: CONGRUOUS : (a. irrelevant, b. compatible, c. reflexive, d. congregated)

17. SUFFICIENT : ENOUGH :: SCARCE : (a. fear, b. hardly, c. few, d. abundant)

18. DIN : NOISE :: CONTORTION : (a. disease, b. writhing, d. exploitation, d. contingency)

19. CONTINENCE : RESTRAINT :: CREVASSE : (a. rift, b. glacier, c. depth, d. mountain)

20. COURTEOUS : URBANE :: EQUITABLE : (a. equine, b. just, c. recurrent, d. ambiguous)

21. FINIAL : PINNACLE :: PEDIMENT : (a. basement, b. footing, c. gable, d. obstruction)

22. TALE : SUPPOSITION :: HISTORY : (a. reality, b. war, c. peace, d. geography)

23. JABBER : GIBBERISH :: QUIDNUNC : (a. quisling, b. gossip, c. theorist, d. testator)

24. KEYNOTE : TONIC :: DIAPASON : (a. diaphragm, b. clef, c. chord, d. organ)

25. BLANCH : PALLOR :: INSTITUTE : (a. form, b. sum, c. purpose, d. begin)

26. CREPUSCULAR : INDISTINCT :: CURSORY : (a. profane, b. egregious, c. superficial, d. unique)

VERBAL ANALOGIES TEST II. ANTONYMS
Time: 13 Minutes. 26 Questions.

Directions: Each of these test questions consists of three CAPITALIZED words and four lettered words enclosed in parentheses. Two of the capitalized words are related in some way. Find the two related words and establish the nature of the relationship. Then study the four words lettered a, b, c and d. Select the one lettered word which is related to the remaining capitalized word in the same way that the first two capitalized words are related. Mark the Answer Sheet for the letter preceding the word you select.

1. SUNDER : CONSOLIDATE :: TANGIBLE : (a. abstract, b. tasty, c. possible, d. tangled)

2. ACCORD : BREACH :: CONNECTION : (a. tie, b. dissociation, c. association, d. distrust)

3. BIRTH : DEATH :: INTRODUCTION : (a. salutations, b. lecturer, c. conclusion, d. prologue)

4. INDIGENT : WEALTHY :: GAUCHE : (a. clumsy, b. clandestine, c. graceful, d. lugubrious)

5. MAGNANIMITY : PARSIMONY :: TOLERANCE : (a. advocation, b. totality, c. urgency, d. bigotry)

6. DERISION : ENCORE :: CATCALL : (a. oblivion, b. meow, c. acceptance, d. backyard)

7. COUNTERFEIT : REAL :: MATURE : (a. spotted, b. rotten, c. unripe, d. grown)

8. INQUISITIVE : INCURIOUS :: MANIFEST : (a. latent, b. many-sided, c. obvious, d. manipulated)

9. IDIOT : GENIUS :: VALLEY : (a. plateau, b. moron, c. mountain, d. field)

10. TEMPORARY : PERMANENT :: EPHEMERAL : (a. elongated, b. useless, c. everlasting, d. heavenly)

11. SPONTANEOUS : CALCULATED :: IMPROMPTU : (a. ad lib, b. memorized, c. verbose, d. prolific)

12. MEDLEY : ONE :: MISCELLANEOUS : (a. collective, b. undetermined, c. righteous, d. single)

13. VALOR : COWARDICE :: WHITE : (a. color, b. dim, c. pigment, d. black)

14. HYPOCRISY : HONESTY :: HOSTILITY : (a. war, b. amity, c. hospital, d. hostage)

15. PLETHORA : DEARTH :: CUNNING : (a. dull, b. earthy, c. foxy, d. cute)

16. INCLEMENT : CLEAR :: PERTINENT : (a. pert, b. cloudy, c. irrelevant, d. perceptive)

17. BRIEF : BOMBASTIC :: LAX : (a. stringent, b. medicinal, c. fishy, d. filthy)

18. SEEK : AVOID :: INDULGE : (a. pursue, b. abstain, c. hunt, d. find)

19. DISHONESTY : INTEGRITY :: OBVIOUS : (a. oblong, b. invidious, c. surreptitious, d. honest)

20. BLASPHEME : REVERE :: COMPREHENSIBLE : (a. composed, b. reprehensible, c. completed, d. inscrutable)

21. COMPETITION : MONOPOLY :: IMMATURITY : (a. anger, b. child, c. adult, d. incompatibility)

22. REPUGN : COMPROMISE :: RESCIND : (a. refuse, b. rest, c. decipher, d. validate)

23. LAUD : DEGRADE :: PRAISE : (a. victory, b. enjoyment, c. criticize, d. succeed)

24. WARLIKE : PEACEFUL :: MARTIAL : (a. military, b. noisy, c. worried, d. halcyon)

25. ENCOURAGE : INTIMIDATE :: ALLOW : (a. interdict, b. comply, c. expect, d. continue)

26. COSTLY : SCARCE :: CHEAP : (a. abundant, b. tinny, c. difficult, d. puny)

VERBAL ANALOGIES TEST III. CAUSE AND EFFECT
Time: 13 Minutes. 26 Questions.

Directions: Each of these test questions consists of three CAPITALIZED words and four lettered words enclosed in parentheses. Two of the capitalized words are related in some way. Find the two related words and establish the nature of the relationship. Then study the four words lettered a, b, c and d. Select the one lettered word which is related to the remaining capitalized word in the same way that the first two capitalized words are related. Mark the Answer Sheet for the letter preceding the word you select.

1. CURIOSITY : ENLIGHTENMENT :: VERACITY : (a. credulousness, b. credibility, c. validity, d. cognizance)

2. LOQUACITY : BOREDOM :: TENACITY : (a. adversity, b. antagonism, c. attainment, d. lassitude)

3. SATISFACTION : GOOD DEED :: IMPROVEMENT : (a. sin, b. fault, c. criticism, d. kindness)

4. SEED : PLANT :: EGG : (a. yolk, b. crack, c. bird, d. shell)

5. ASSIDUITY : SUCCESS :: CARE : (a. avoidance, b. accident, c. fruition, d. safety)

6. WHEAT : FLOUR :: GRAPE : (a. vintage, b. vine, c. wine, d. fruit)

7. GRIEF : WAR :: HAPPINESS : (a. joy, b. peace, c. soldier, d. finish)

8. MOON : LIGHT :: ECLIPSE : (a. violence, b. darkness, c. cruelty, d. whistling)

9. HEAT : FIRE :: WATER : (a. sky, b. rain, c. lake, d. H_2O)

10. WOUND : BLOOD :: ACCIDENT : (a. damage, b. case, c. car, d. murder)

11. HEALTH : SANITATION :: DISEASE : (a. filthy, b. measles, c. carelessness, d. illness)

12. RETARDATION : DISPARAGEMENT :: ACCELERATION : (a. motor, b. encouragement, c. rapidity, d. calmness)

13. LAZINESS : FAILURE :: STRATEGY : (a. mentality, b. brutality, c. company, d. victory)

14. AIR : SUFFOCATION :: FOOD : (a. starvation, b. indigestion, c. energy, d. life)

15. PREDICAMENT : CARELESSNESS :: RESPONSE : (a. answer, b. stimulus, c. correct, d. effect)

16. FALL : PAIN :: DISOBEDIENCE : (a. punishment, b. crime, c. defiance, d. distress)

17. AIMLESSNESS : DELINQUENCY :: BOREDOM : (a. inadequacy, b. mischief, c. meditation, d. discord)

18. BIGOTRY : HATRED :: FANATICISM : (a. revolution, b. criticism, c. intolerance, d. enthusiasm)

19. GUILT : CONVICTION :: INNOCENCE : (a. revenge, b. contrition, c. justice, d. vindication)

20. LIQUOR : ALCOHOLISM :: CANDY : (a. confectionery, b. blemish, c. obesity, d. overindulgence)

21. RAIN : FLOODING :: ICE : (a. freezing, b. skidding, c. snowing, d. skating)

22. FIRE : SMOKE :: PROFLIGACY : (a. debt, b. disappearance, c. dispersal, d. deceit)

23. FOOD : GROWTH :: WORK : (a. employment, b. entertainment, c. office, d. income)

24. INEXPERIENCE : ERROR :: CARELESSNESS : (a. recklessness, b. caution, c. indifference, d. accident)

25. IMPLACABILITY : DISCORD :: DISHONESTY : (a. disinterest, b. dissent, c. distrust, d. mendacity)

26. FLAME : BURN :: INSULT : (a. disdain, b. anger, c. approbation, d. reparation)

VERBAL ANALOGIES TEST IV. PART TO WHOLE
Time: 13 Minutes. 26 Questions.

Directions: Each of these test questions consists of three CAPITALIZED words and four lettered words enclosed in parentheses. Two of the capitalized words are related in some way. Find the two related words and establish the nature of the relationship. Then study the four words lettered a, b, c and d. Select the one lettered word which is related to the remaining capitalized word in the same way that the first two capitalized words are related. Mark the Answer Sheet for the letter preceding the word you select.

1. VERSAILLES : PALACE :: BASTILLE : (a. parkway, b. Paris, c. prison, d. France)

2. PLAY : PROLOGUE :: CONSTITUTION : (a. preamble, b. laws, c. Washington, d. country)

3. PARAGRAPH : SENTENCE :: SENTENCE : (a. clause, b. word, c. composition. d. correctness)

4. NECKLACE : BEAD :: CHAIN : (a. ball, b. iron, c. link, d. strength)

5. PIT : PEACH :: SUN : (a. planet, b. moon, c. orbit, d. solar system)

6. SLICE : LOAF :: ISLAND : (a. land, b. archipelago, c. peninsula, d. ocean)

7. MOUNTAIN : PEAK :: WAVE : (a. water, b. storm, c. crest, d. ocean)

8. STEER : RANCH :: MEAT : (a. carpenter, b. market, c. roast, d. cowboy)

9. INGREDIENT : RECIPE :: YELLOW : (a. yolk, b. green, c. liver, d. age)

10. STONE : QUARRY :: LUMBER : (a. crystalization, b. mine, c. foliage, d. forest)

11. COPPER : ORE :: MARBLE : (a. granite, b. hardness, c. limestone, d. sculpture)

12. STEEL : COMPOUND :: IRON : (a. compound, b. element, c. alloy, d. mixture)

13. BEE : STINGER :: MAN : (a. wound, b. woman, c. fist, d. shield)

14. WHOLE : PART :: CANADA : (a. United States, b. Lake Erie, c. Ontario, d. North America)

15. CRATER : VOLCANO :: CHIMNEY : (a. fire, b. house, c. fuel, d. smoke)

16. BOOK : PREFACE :: HOTEL : (a. room, b. guest, c. manager, d. lobby)

17. TOASTMASTER : BANQUET :: CHAIRMAN : (a. speaker, b. orator, c. assembly, d. speech)

18. AIRPLANE : PARACHUTE :: BOAT : (a. rescue, b. sink, c. life preserver, d. safety)

19. PETAL : FLOWER :: FUR : (a. coat, b. rabbit, c. warm, d. women)

20. CHEMISTRY : ELEMENTS :: GRAMMAR : (a. teacher, b. English, c. subject, d. parts of speech)

21. WOOD : TABLE :: STEEL : (a. chair, b. iron, c. lumber, d. knife)

22. CARROT : PLANT :: COW : (a. meat, b. herd, c. animal, d. stockyard)

23. PRESIDENT : CORPORATION :: GOVERNOR : (a. mayor, b. state, c. nation, d. government)

24. PLAYER : TEAM :: EAR : (a. face, b. eye, c. head, d. brain)

25. CHINESE : MONGOLIAN : ENGLISH : (a. Danish, b. race, c. Caucasian, d. language)

26. WINE : DREGS :: WHEAT : (a. bushel, b. chaff, c. stalk, d. bread)

VERBAL ANALOGIES TEST V. PART TO PART
Time: 13 Minutes. 26 Questions.

Directions: Each of these test questions consists of three CAPITALIZED words and four lettered words enclosed in parentheses. Two of the capitalized words are related in some way. Find the two related words and establish the nature of the relationship. Then study the four words lettered a, b, c and d. Select the one lettered word which is related to the remaining capitalized word in the same way that the first two capitalized words are related. Mark the Answer Sheet for the letter preceding the word you select.

1. NEPHEW : NIECE :: UNCLE : (a. man, b. relative, c. father, d. aunt)

2. HAND : ELBOW :: FOOT : (a. muscle, b. knee, c. leg, d. toe)

3. MATURITY : ADOLESCENCE :: CHILDHOOD : (a. manhood, b. infancy, c. school, d. immaturity)

4. BARITONE : TENOR :: CONTRALTO : (a. opera, b. soprano, c. woman, d. song)

5. DAUGHTER : MOTHER :: SON : (a. child, b. grandfather, c. boy, d. father)

6. HEAD : HAT :: FOOT : (a. toe, b. leg, c. anatomy, d. shoe)

7. TABLE : CLOTH :: BED : (a. blanket, b. mattress, c. pillow, d. spread)

8. SALESMAN : PRODUCT :: TEACHER : (a. principal, b. English, c. pupils, d. subject)

9. PUPIL : TEACHER :: CHILD : (a. parent, b. dolly, c. youngster, d. obey)

10. ARM : LEG :: FLIPPER : (a. wing, b. tail, c. head, d. whale)

11. MINNOW : SHARK :: PUPPY : (a. elephant, b. whale, c. wolfhound, d. mastodon)

12. CARROT : LETTUCE :: POTATO : (a. grape, b. cabbage, c. radish, d. onion)

13. COACH : PLAYER :: COUNSELOR : (a. tutor, b. supervisor, c. leader, d. camper)

14. CUBE : PYRAMID :: SQUARE : (a. box, b. Egypt, c. pentagon, d. triangle)

15. GANDER : GOOSE :: BULL : (a. cow, b. hog, c. pig, d. lamb)

16. TRACTOR : HANDPLOW :: ELEVATOR : (a. building, b. skyscraper, c. stairs, d. feet)

17. INCH : MILE :: HUT : (a. foundation, b. skyscraper, c. building, d. abode)

18. MOON : EARTH :: EARTH : (a. Mars, b. moon, c. sky, d. sun)

19. EWE : RAM :: MARE : (a. cow, b. antelope, c. calf, d. stallion)

20. OAK : ACORN :: VINE : (a. shoot, b. grape, c. creeper, d. bower)

21. SETTING : STONE :: SOCKET : (a. eye, b. bulb, c. lamp, d. light)

22. GELDING : STALLION :: CAPON : (a. hen, b. fowl, c. bird, d. rooster)

23. EYE : EAR :: SHIRT : (a. button, b. pants, c. cotton, d. clothing)

24. TOE : FINGER :: HEEL : (a. shoe, b. foot, c. sole, d. limb)

25. BUTTON : SEAM :: HEADLIGHT : (a. car, b. bicycle, c. bumper, d. night)

26. WING : BEAK :: PAW : (a. tail, b. foot, c. cat, d. dog)

VERBAL ANALOGIES TEST VI. PURPOSE
Time: 13 Minutes. 26 Questions.

Directions: Each of these test questions consists of three CAPITALIZED words and four lettered words enclosed in parentheses. Two of the capitalized words are related in some way. Find the two related words and establish the nature of the relationship. Then study the four words lettered a, b, c and d. Select the one lettered word which is related to the remaining capitalized word in the same way that the first two capitalized words are related. Mark the Answer Sheet for the letter preceding the word you select.

1. HORSE : HITCHING POST :: CRAFT : (a. parapet, b. moorage, c. running, d. vessel)

2. BALL : BAT :: SHUTTLECOCK : (a. battledore, b. badminton, c. plumage, d. game)

3. AIRPLANE : TRANSPORTATION :: WIRELESS : (a. message, b. speed, c. transoceanic, d. communication)

4. CALF : SHOE :: GOOSE : (a. gander, b. pillow, c. roast, d. feathers)

5. WINDOW : CURTAIN :: TABLE : (a. wood, b. chair, c. house, d. cloth)

6. GYMNASIUM : EXERCISE :: THEATER : (a. act, b. drama, c. stage, d. performance)

7. ETYMOLOGY : WORDS :: HAGIOLOGY : (a. saints, b. senility, c. selling, d. writing)

8. FOOTBALL : SIGNALS :: WAR : (a. guns, b. codes, c. peace, d. soldiers)

9. FINGER : TACTILE :: NOSE : (a. proboscis, b. smell, c. olfactory, d. redolent)

10. ARCHAEOLOGIST : ANTIQUITY :: ICHTHYOLOGIST : (a. theology, b. marine life, c. horticulture, d. mysticism)

11. PORK : PIG :: MUTTON : (a. wool, b. sheep, c. animal, d. farm)

12. PRESS : PRINT :: ERASER : (a. efface, b. board, c. chalk, d. rubber)

13. THIRST : WATER :: HUNGER : (a. starving, b. eat, c. drink, d. food)

14. MENU : MEAL :: MAP : (a. road, b. distance, c. trip, d. scale)

15. AX : WOODSMAN :: AWL : (a. cut, b. hew, plumber, d. cobbler)

16. SURGEON : SCALPEL :: BUTCHER : (a. mallet, b. cleaver, c. chisel, d. wrench)

17. GUN : HOLSTER :: SWORD : (a. pistol, b. scabbard, c. warrior, d. slay)

18. LETTER CARRIER : MAIL :: MESSENGER : (a. value, b. dispatches, c. easy, d. complicated)

19. BANDAGE : WOUND :: STRING : (a. package, b. sling, c. rope, d. twine)

20. LIQUID : SIPHON :: SMOKE : (a. tobacco, b. fire, c. flame, d. flue)

21. MAN : BREAD :: HORSE : (a. stable, b. duck, c. barn, d. hay)

22. CARPENTER : SAW :: MASON : (a. house, b. wall, c. man, d. trowel)

23. BARREL : WINE :: SILO : (a. horses, b. floss, c. grain, d. refuse)

24. BRICK : BUILDING :: LEATHER : (a. steer, b. hide, c. belt, d. calf)

25. MASK : FACE :: HELMET : (a. steel, b. head, c. combat, d. football)

26. PHOTOGRAPH : SOUVENIR :: MOVIE : (a. theater, b. star, c. entertainment, d. actors)

VERBAL ANALOGIES TEST VII. ACTION TO OBJECT
Time: 13 Minutes. 26 Questions.

Directions: Each of these test questions consists of three CAPI-TALIZED words and four lettered words enclosed in parentheses. Two of the capitalized words are related in some way. Find the two related words and establish the nature of the relationship. Then study the four words lettered a, b, c and d. Select the one lettered word which is related to the remaining capitalized word in the same way that the first two capitalized words are related. Mark the Answer Sheet for the letter preceding the word you select.

1. HEAR : SOUND :: SEE : (a. move, b. taste, c. picture, d. vision)

2. OBEY : CHILDREN :: COMMAND : (a. performance, b. parents, c. army, d. result)

3. BARK : DOG :: ROAR : (a. lion, b. snake, c. lamb, d. train)

4. ACT : ACTRESS :: SING : (a. vocalist, b. singing, c. chorus, d. music)

5. SCRUB : FLOOR :: SCOUR : (a. sweep, b. pan, c. kitchen, d. cleanse)

6. PEEL : BANANA :: SHELL : (a. sea, b. fish, c. sand, d. oyster)

7. BEHEAD : GUILLOTINE :: HANG : (a. gallows, b. nail, c. murderer, d. picture)

8. ALTERATION : GARMENT :: REVISION : (a. book, b. remodeling, c. correction, d. content)

9. VIEW : SCENE :: HEAR : (a. taste, b. concert, c. odor, d. color)

10. WALKS : MAN :: SWIMS : (a. fish, b. pool, c. pier, d. boat)

11. STUDY : LEARN :: TRY : (a. begin, b. attempt, c. tail, d. succeed)

12. HEAL : PHYSICIAN :: LEND : (a. money, b. banker, c. owe, d. give)

13. SPEECH : MAN :: SONG : (a. ditty, b. bird, c. sheep, d. tune)

14. POLISH : MANICURIST :: POLISH : (a. bootblack, b. shoe, c. buff, d. nail)

15. EVADE : PURSUER :: DODGE : (a. ball, b. car, c. escape, d. blow)

16. EAT : BREAD :: WEAR : (a. store, b. coat, c. wool, d. sheep)

17. WHET : APPETITE :: HONE : (a. hunger, b. knife, c. meal, d. fork)

18. REIGN : KING :: PRESIDE : (a. court, b. jury, c. judge, d. subject)

19. RACE : TRACK :: SWIM : (a. stroke, b. breathe, c. meet, d. pool)

20. DISCREDIT : CHEAT :: ADMIRE : (a. valiant, b. honor, c. hero, d. daring)

21. OVERLOOK : MISTAKE :: ADVOCATE : (a. recommend, b. cause, c. consider, d. error)

22. WITHER : BLOOM :: PASS : (a. time, b. study, c. fail, d. excuse)

23. ARTICULATE : DESIRE :: ASSUAGE : (a. appease, b. reassure, c. fear, d. joy)

24. ASSIMILATE : KNOWLEDGE :: ASSUME : (a. culture, b. erudition, c. deception, d. debt)

25. THWART : ASPIRATIONS :: STIFLE : (a. heat, b. air, c. anger, d. sense)

26. DREDGE : SILT :: SCOOP : (a. ice cream, b. ladle, c. shovel, d. newspaper)

VERBAL ANALOGIES TEST VIII. OBJECT TO ACTION
Time: 13 Minutes. 26 Questions.

Directions: Each of these test questions consists of three CAPITALIZED words and four lettered words enclosed in parentheses. Two of the capitalized words are related in some way. Find the two related words and establish the nature of the relationship. Then study the four words lettered a, b, c and d. Select the one lettered word which is related to the remaining capitalized word in the same way that the first two capitalized words are related. Mark the Answer Sheet for the letter preceding the word you select.

1. RASCAL : LIE :: GENTLEMAN : (a. friend, b. reply, c. lady, d. truth)

2. ENEMY : HATE :: FRIEND : (a. reject, b. contend, c. love, d. reply)

3. MISTAKE : ERASER :: CONSTITUTION :: (a. preamble, b. amendment, c. law, d. independence)

4. PSYCHIATRIST : MALADJUSTMENT :: DOCTOR : (a. operation, b. disease, c. poverty, d. therapy)

5. CHECK : FORGERY :: COPYRIGHT : (a. bank, b. infringement, c. book, d. author)

6. MAN : OMNIVOROUS :: LION : (a. kingly, b. animal, c. carnivorous, d. omnipotent)

7. PHYSICS : MOTION :: PHYSIOLOGY : (a. function, b. geology, c. Newton, d. Pasteur)

8. TAILOR : PATTERN :: ARCHITECT : (a. house, b. drawing board, c. plan, d. artist)

9. PAST : REGRET :: FUTURE : (a. miss, b. hope, c. anticipate, d. foretell)

10. SHIP : MUTINY :: ARMY : (a. court-martial, b. desertion, c. officer, d. navy)

11. REFEREE : RULES :: CONSCIENCE : (a. thought, b. regulations, c. morals, d. Freud)

12. WOOD : DECAY :: IRON : (a. dampness, b. rust, c. steel, d. ore)

13. DIAGNOSIS : ANALYSIS :: THESIS : (a. college, b. research, c. library, d. paper)

14. WATER : IRRIGATION :: AIR : (a. oxygen, b. respiration, c. ventilation, d. atmosphere)

15. DISHES : BREAK :: CLOTHING : (a. wardrobe, b. tear, c. silverware, d. fall)

16. TONE : HEARING :: COLOR : (a. pigment, b. sight, c. melody, d. picture)

17. KNIFE : GRIND :: STOCKING : (a. wear, b. tear, c. see, d. darn)

18. CONCERT : RECORD :: LANDSCAPE :: (a. photograph, b. artist, c. countryside, d. tree)

19. CANVAS : PAINT :: CLAY : (a. mold, b. cloth, c. statue, d. art)

20. PLAY : REHEARSAL :: GAME : (a. football, b. practice, c. coach, d. players)

21. SEED : SOW :: EGG : (a. pollinate, b. hatch, c. plant, d. fruit)

22. SALT : MINE :: MARBLE : (a. palace, b. engraving, d. stone, d. quarry)

23. FEE : PAY :: GRAIN : (a. eat, b. sew, c. wheat, d. sow)

24. COMPOSER : MUSIC :: AUTHOR : (a. typewriter, b. book, c. dramatist, d. character)

25. ARMY : RECRUIT :: RELIGION : (a. priest, b. worshiper, c. convert, d. church)

26. PROFIT : SELLING :: FAME : (a. buying, b. cheating, c. bravery, d. praying)

VERBAL ANALOGIES TEST IX. PLACE
Time: 13 Minutes. 26 Questions.

Directions: Each of these test questions consists of three CAPITALIZED words and four lettered words enclosed in parentheses. Two of the capitalized words are related in some way. Find the two related words and establish the nature of the relationship. Then study the four words lettered a, b, c and d. Select the one lettered word which is related to the remaining capitalized word in the same way that the first two capitalized words are related. Mark the Answer Sheet for the letter preceding the word you select.

1. THIMBLE : FINGER :: SOCK : (a. band, b. felt, c. hat rack, d. foot)

2. PEASANT : HOVEL :: KING : (a. queen, b. royalty, c. crown, d. palace)

3. COUNTRY : RAILROADS :: BODY : (a. arteries, b. hands, c. brain, d. muscles)

4. MONEY : BANK :: KNOWLEDGE : (a. intelligence, b. blackboard, c. books, d. graduation)

5. BOOKS : LIBRARY :: WHEAT : (a. oats, b. granary, c. breakfast, d. field)

6. REVOLUTION : LAND :: MUTINY : (a. captain, b. mutilate, c. bounty, d. sea)

7. VINE : MELON :: TREE : (a. limb, b. leaf, c. pear, d. earth)

8. SUBMARINE : FISH :: AIRPLANE : (a. aquarium, b. bird, c. wing, d. hangar)

9. WATER : AQUEDUCT :: BLOOD : (a. corpuscle, b. body, c. vein, d. plasma)

10. FRANC : FRANCE :: PESO : (a. pizza, b. Mexico, c. pestle, d. England)

11. PENINSULA : MAINLAND :: FIORD : (a. boats, b. bay, c. sea, d. Massachusetts)

12. ILLINOIS : CHICAGO :: MASSACHUSETTS : (a. Boston, b. Kentucky, c. New York, d. Europe)

13. COUNTRY : ARGENTINA :: STATE : (a. earth, b. Asia, c. Boston, d. Idaho)

14. WATER : AIR :: BOAT : (a. sail, b. sea, c. yacht, d. plane)

15. BABY :: CARRIAGE : MAN : (a. woman, b. automobile, c. child, d. adult)

16. ENGLAND : LONDON :: CANADA : (a. Montreal, b. Ontario, c. Quebec, d. Banff)

17. HOSPITAL : NURSE :: SCHOOL : (a. lawyer, b. apple, c. test, d. teacher)

18. AUTOMOBILE : TRAIN :: CHAUFFEUR : (a. engineer, b. driver, c. butler, d. servant)

19. SCOTLAND : BAGPIPE :: SPAIN : (a. harp, b. guitar, c. piano, d. trumpet)

20. CAPE : CONTINENT :: GULF : (a. ocean, b. lake, c. reservoir, d. water)

21. GYMNASIUM : HEALTH :: LIBRARY : (a. sick, b. school, c. books, d. knowledge)

22. RUSSIA : STEPPES :: ARGENTINA : (a. mountains, b. pampas, c. plateaus, d. valleys)

23. OFFICE : TYPIST :: FACTORY : (a. mechanic, b. machinery, c. smoke, d. production)

24. FACULTY : UNIVERSITY :: STAFF : (a. intern, b. stretcher, c. beds, d. hospital)

25. BAY : OCEAN :: PENINSULA : (a. continent, b. sea, c. gulf, d. island)

26. STATION : TRAIN :: WHARF : (a. steamer, b. pier, c. water, d. river)

VERBAL ANALOGIES TEST X. ASSOCIATION
Time: 13 Minutes. 26 Questions.

Directions: Each of these test questions consists of three CAPI-TALIZED words and four lettered words enclosed in parentheses. Two of the capitalized words are related in some way. Find the two related words and establish the nature of the relationship. Then study the four words lettered a, b, c and d. Select the one lettered word which is related to the remaining capitalized word in the same way that the first two capitalized words are related. Mark the Answer Sheet for the letter preceding the word you select.

1. SILK : RAYON :: BUTTER : (a. margarine, b. oil, c. cream, d. bread)

2. GUEST : ACCEPTANCE :: HOST : (a. party, b. hostess, c. refreshments, d. invitation)

3. FOOD : NUTRITION :: LIGHT : (a. vision, b. bulb, c. electricity, d. watt)

4. SERVICE : FEE :: FAVOR : (a. deed, b. request, c. person, d. thanks)

5. WATER : RUBBER :: FIRE : (a. ashes, b. heat, c. asbestos, d. melting)

6. INFANTRY : FOOT :: CAVALRY :: (a. horse, b. hoof, c. neigh, d. army)

7. PRESENT : BIRTHDAY :: REWARD : (a. accomplishment, b. punishment, c. medal, d. money)

8. BALLET : TERPSICHORE :: POETRY : (a. Zeus, b. Achilles, c. Mt. Olympus, d. Erato)

9. LAWBREAKER : BAIL :: HOSTAGE : (a. criminal, b. ransom, c. murder, d. threat)

10. VICTORY : CONTEST :: KNOWLEDGE : (a. professor, b. test, c. degree, d. study)

11. MONARCHY : KING :: DEMOCRACY : (a. vote, b. freedom, c. people, d. republic)

12. SOLUTION : MYSTERY :: LEARNING : (a. study, b. comics, c. college, d. school)

13. WEALTH : MERCENARY :: GOLD : (a. Midas, b. mine, c. fame, d. South Africa)

14. TEARS : SORROW :: LAUGHTER : (a. joy, b. smile, c. girls, d. grain)

15. HONOR : BRAVERY :: GUILT : (a. thief, b. crime, c. jail, d. killer)

16. BIBLIOPHILE : BOOKS :: PHILATELIST : (a. pharmacy, b. coins, c. stamps, d. jewelry)

17. NAIAD : WATER :: DRYAD : (a. land, b. tree, c. elm, d. wringer)

18. FAMINE : FOOD :: DROUGHT : (a. river, b. irrigation, c. dam, d. water)

19. GOLD : YELLOW :: ROYAL : (a. pink, b. white, c. black, d. blue)

20. THIRTEEN : THREE ON A MATCH :: IDES OF MARCH : (a. will-o'-the-wisp, b. broken mirror, c. Scapa Flow, d. cat-o'-nine-tails)

21. HALF-MAST : ELEGY :: DAWN : (a. return, b. speech, c. inception, d. plot)

22. FEVER : SPRING :: LEAVES : (a. October, b. autumn, c. season, d. sadness)

23. SILENTS : TALKIES :: RADIO : (a. tube, b. broadcast, c. television, d. space travel)

24. ECUMENICAL : CHURCH :: CULINARY : (a. bedroom, b. closet, c. knife, d. kitchen)

25. PENNANT : TEAM :: OSCAR : (a. teacher, b. player, c. actor, d. surgeon)

26. MIDAS : BRYAN :: GOLD : (a. silver, b. politician, c. miser, d. men)

VERBAL ANALOGIES TEST XI. SEQUENCE
Time: 13 Minutes. 26 Questions.

Directions: Each of these test questions consists of three CAPITALIZED words and four lettered words enclosed in parentheses. Two of the capitalized words are related in some way. Find the two related words and establish the nature of the relationship. Then study the four words lettered a, b, c and d. Select the one lettered word which is related to the remaining capitalized word in the same way that the first two capitalized words are related. Mark the Answer Sheet for the letter preceding the word you select.

1. MAY : FEBRUARY :: NOVEMBER : (a. August, b. January, c. October, d. July)

2. THIRD : FIRST :: JEFFERSON : (a. Washington, b. White House, c. president, d. Jackson)

3. Q : M :: G : (a. K, b. C, c. D, d. F)

4. ABD : EFH :: IJL : (a. MNO, b. NOP, c. NOO, d. MNP)

5. TUESDAY : THURSDAY :: SATURDAY : (a. Sunday, b. Monday, c. Wednesday, d. Friday)

6. MIDDLE AGES : RENAISSANCE :: 1700 : (a. Dark Ages, b. 1500, c. ancient Greece, d. 20th century)

7. WINTER : AUTUMN :: SUMMER : (a. month, b. spring, c. solstice, d. climate)

8. SHEEP : LAMB :: DOG : (a. bone, b. bark, c. pup, d. kennel)

9. TODAY : YESTERDAY :: PRESENT : (a. yesterday, b. Monday, c. past, d. gift)

10. COLT : STALLION :: STREAM : (a. water, b. river, c. brook, d. puddle)

11. HOUR : MINUTE :: MINUTE : (a. time, b. day, c. second, d. moment)

12. SENILITY : CHILDHOOD :: DUSK : (a. twilight, b. dawn, c. night, d. rain)

13. WINTER : SPRING :: DEATH : (a. end, b. continuation, c. birth, d. sorrow)

14. APRIL : JUNE :: JANUARY : (a. month, b. March, c. February, d. beginning)

15. CENTURY : DECADE :: DIME : (a. lucre, b. cent, c. age, d. nickel)

16. INTERN : PHYSICIAN :: APPRENTICE : (a. doctor, b. lawyer, c. journeyman, d. craftsman)

17. ACORN : OAK :: INFANT : (a. individual, b. baby, c. adult, d. male)

18. MONTH : WEEK :: WEEK : (a. day, b. month, c. year, d. hour)

19. TOMORROW : YESTERDAY :: FUTURE : (a. present, b. unknown, c. year, d. past)

20. SECOND : FOURTH :: B : (a. A, b. D, c. Q, d. C)

21. COKE : COAL :: BREAD : (a. eat, b. money, c. dough, d. yeast)

22. WEEK : DAY :: DAY : (a. month, b. second, c. hour, d. night)

23. INCH : SQUARE INCH :: SQUARE INCH : (a. inch, b. cubic inch, c. foot, d. yard)

24. MARE : FILLY :: KING : (a. throne, b. prince, c. kingdom, d. majesty)

25. BUD : FLOWER :: SCRATCH : (a. thorn, b. scar, c. amputation, d. fever)

26. QUART : PINT :: GALLON : (a. inch, b. gram, c. liter, d. quart)

VERBAL ANALOGIES TEST XII. CHARACTERISTIC
Time: 13 Minutes. 26 Questions.

Directions: Each of these test questions consists of three CAPI-TALIZED words and four lettered words enclosed in parentheses. Two of the capitalized words are related in some way. Find the two related words and establish the nature of the relationship. Then study the four words lettered a, b, c and d. Select the one lettered word which is related to the remaining capitalized word in the same way that the first two capitalized words are related. Mark the Answer Sheet for the letter preceding the word you select.

1. RICH : OWN :: WISE : (a. know, b. teach, c. divulge, d. save)

2. DOVE : PEACE :: BEAVER : (a. coat, b. industry, c. fur, d. mammal)

3. DETECTIVE : CLUES :: SCIENTIST : (a. chemicals, b. books, c. experiments, d. facts)

4. COMMON : IRON :: RARE : (a. steak, b. crowd, c. humor, d. diamond)

5. MISER : MONEY :: HERMIT : (a. complaining, b. weakness, c. insistence, d. solitude)

6. AUDIBLE : NOISE :: VISIBLE : (a. picture, b. honesty, c. distance, d. heaven)

7. PILOT : ALERT :: MARKSMAN : (a. strong, b. cruel, c. kind, d. steady)

8. LOUD : THUNDER :: LARGE : (a. monkey, b. midget, c. whale, d. blatancy)

9. DEPRESSION : DESPAIR :: CHEER : (a. victory, b. hope, c. gloom, d. celebration

10. SWEET : SUGAR :: BITTER : (a. malaria, b. quinine, c. saccharine, d. acidity)

11. FEVER : SICKNESS :: CLOUD : (a. sky, b. cold, c. storm, d. weather)

12. NOISE : DISTRACTING :: HARMONY : (a. harmful, b. loud, c. orchestrated, d. pleasing)

13. GASTRONOMICAL : GOURMET :: GEOLOGICAL : (a. raconteur, b. entomologist, c. etymologist, d. paleontologist)

14. STREAM : MEANDERING :: HIGHWAY : (a. traffic, b. direct, c. speed, d. distance)

15. SNOW : WINTER :: RAIN : (a. wet, b. summer, c. cold, d. flood)

16. NOVICE : INSECURITY :: EXPERT : (a. tools, b. confidence, c. difficulty, d. money)

17. RUST : IRON :: MOLD : (a. bread, b. penicillin, c. virus, d. disease)

18. SINKS : ROCK :: FLOATS : (a. feather, b. light, c. flies, d. drowns)

19. FOX : CUNNING :: SAGE : (a. brains, b. student, c. school, d. wisdom)

20. CORK : BUOYANT :: DIAMOND : (a. jewel, b. watch, c. brilliant, d. extravagant)

21. POETRY : VERSE :: JOURNALISM : (a. extemporaneous, b. current, c. prose, d. terse)

22. DESERT : ARID :: TUNDRA : (a. exotic, b. dry, c. salty, d. frozen)

23. INGENUE : NAIVETY :: KNAVE : (a. chivalry, b. chicanery, c. morality, d. subtlety)

24. PRESCIENCE : SEER :: PREJUDICE : (a. Hispanic, b. Black, c. minority, d. bigot)

25. HERO : VALOR :: HERETIC : (a. dissent, b. bravado, c. reverence, d. discretion)

26. RESILIENT : BALL :: RESONANT : (a. loud, b. resounding, c. response, d. echo)

VERBAL ANALOGIES TEST XIII. DEGREE
Time: 13 Minutes. 26 Questions.

Directions: Each of these test questions consists of three CAPI-TALIZED words and four lettered words enclosed in parentheses. Two of the capitalized words are related in some way. Find the two related words and establish the nature of the relationship. Then study the four words lettered a, b, c and d. Select the one lettered word which is related to the remaining capitalized word in the same way that the first two capitalized words are related. Mark the Answer Sheet for the letter preceding the word you select.

1. POSSIBLE : PROBABLE :: HOPE : (a. expect, b. deceive, c. resent, d. prove)

2. GRAY : BLACK :: DISCOMFORT : (a. green, b. pain, c. hospital, d. mutilation)

3. ORATION : CHAT :: BANQUET : (a. festival, b. party, c. ball, d. snack)

4. MOTORCYCLE : BICYCLE :: AUTOMOBILE : (a. bus, b. airplane, c. transportation, d. wagon)

5. SHOWER : CLOUDBURST :: BREEZE : (a. rain, b. sunshine, c. climate, d. cyclone)

6. INFANT : ADULT :: KITTEN : (a. dog, b. cat, c. pig, d. giraffe)

7. HUMMINGBIRD : EAGLE :: SHRUB : (a. forest, b. mountain, c. grass, d. tree)

8. FLEA : HORSEFLY :: MINNOW : (a. eagle, b. whale, c. giant, d. elephant)

9. AUTOMOBILE : HORSE :: TELEGRAM : (a. telephone, b. letter, c. communication, d. transportation)

10. GUN : CLUB :: HOUSE : (a. prehistoric, b. cave, c. cannon, d. rampage)

11. MIST : SLEET :: SIP : (a. swallow, b. gulp, c. chew, d. devour)

12. BEG : PLEAD :: ALMS : (a. beggar, b. selfishness, c. charity, d. philanthropist)

13. WALK : LIMP :: TALK : (a. pronunciation, b. stammer, c. crutch, d. speech)

14. NONE : LITTLE :: NEVER : (a. sometimes, b. frequently, c. negative, d. seldom)

15. WORST : WORSE :: WORSE : (a. bad, b. good, c. best, d. better)

16. STEAM : WATER :: WATER : (a. heat, b. molecules, c. ice, d. matter)

17. DEMONIC : NAUGHTY :: RAGE : (a. irk, b. annoy, c. anger, d. mischief)

18. INFANT : TODDLER :: BOY : (a. man, b. youth, c. adult, d. masculine)

19. SMILE : LAUGH :: WASH : (a. bathe, b. lather, c. water, d. dry)

20. WALK : RUN :: ADD : (a. number, b. total, c. multiply, d. subtract)

21. TRICKLE : GUSH :: TEPID : (a. torpid, b. torrid, c. frigid, d. comfortable)

22. SKIM : SCAN :: PERUSE : (a. study, b. understand, c. interpret, d. predict)

23. SUGGEST : RECOMMEND :: ESTIMATE : (a. guess, b. value, c. calculate, d. worth)

24. DRONE : DECLAIM :: PRAISE : (a. exhort, b. exclaim, c. extort, d. extol)

25. EDICT : DIRECTIVE :: GALLANT : (a. splendid, b. civil, c. spirited, d. court'y)

26. GRIEF : DISTRESS :: COVET : (a. acquire, b. want, c. possess, d. pretext)

VERBAL ANALOGIES TEST XIV. GRAMMATICAL
Time: 13 Minutes. 26 Questions.

Directions: Each of these test questions consists of three CAPI-TALIZED words and four lettered words enclosed in parentheses. Two of the capitalized words are related in some way. Find the two related words and establish the nature of the relationship. Then study the four words lettered a, b, c and d. Select the one lettered word which is related to the remaining capitalized word in the same way that the first two capitalized words are related. Mark the Answer Sheet for the letter preceding the word you select.

1. SPRING : SPRUNG :: LIE : (a. lie, b. lain, c. lies, d. lay)

2. ROSE : RISE :: WENT : (a. going, b. gone, c. go, d. return)

3. SHABBY : SHABBILY :: HARMONIOUS : (a. harp, b. harmonica, c. harmoniously, d. harmony)

4. PLAUSIBILITY : PLAUSIBLE :: INFAMY : (a. infamous, b. inflammatory, c. infernal, d. unfamiliar)

5. ITS : BABIES' :: THEIR : (a. you, b. your, c. ladies, d. we)

6. SHEEP : EWE :: ALUMNUS : (a. alumna, b. alumni, c. alum, d. alumnas)

7. DONKEY : DONKEYS :: MOUSE : (a. mouses, b. mice, c. rats, d. trap)

8. MOOSE : MOOSE :: I : (a. mine, b. they, c. us, d. we)

9. LIES : LAIN :: DRINKS : (a. drunk, b. drink, c. drinked, d. drank)

10. HE : HIM :: WE : (a. me, b. us, c. them, d. you)

11. THREE : THIRD :: ONE : (a. fourth, b. third, c. second, d. first)

12. SPEAK : SPOKE :: TELL : (a. sang, b. talk, c. told, d. singing)

13. REVERT : REVERSION :: SYMPATHIZE : (a. sympathetic, b. symposium, c. sympathy, d. sympathizer)

14. CAPT. : CAPTAIN :: LB. : (a. building, b. oz., c. pound, d. ton)

15. DOWN : DOWNY :: AGE : (a. aging, b. old, c. ancient, d. historic)

16. I : MINE :: MAN : (a. men, b. his, c. man's, d. mine)

17. REGRESSIVE : REGRESS :: STERILE : (a. sterilization, b. sterilize, c. sterility, d. sterilizer)

18. LAY : LIES :: ATE : (a. eaten, b. eats, c. eating, d. eat)

19. E'ER : NE'ER :: THEY'RE : (a. their, b. your, c. we're, d. one's)

20. MINE : YOURS :: HIS : (a. its, b. it's, c. her's, d. their's)

21. RELIEF : BELIEVE :: RECEIVE : (a. friend, b. deceit, c. belief, d. brief)

22. MEDIUM : MEDIA :: LEAF : (a. leafs, b. leave, c. left, d. leaves)

23. LIFE : LIVES :: BROTHER-IN-LAW : (a. brother-in-laws, b. brothers-in-law, c. brother-in-law's, d. brother's-in-law)

24. BRING : BROUGHT :: WRITE : (a. wrought, b. writer, c. writing, d. wrote)

25. ANALYSIS : ANALYSES :: RADIUS : (a. radii, b. radial, c. radices, d. radiums)

26. SIMPLE : SIMPLEST :: MANY : (a. fewest, b. myriad, c. more, d. most)

CORRECT ANSWERS FOR ANALOGY TESTS
CLASSIFIED BY CATEGORY

TEST I. SYNONYMS

1. d	5. d	9. c	13. a	17. c	21. c	25. d
2. c	6. d	10. d	14. b	18. b	22. a	26. c
3. b	7. a	11. a	15. d	19. a	23. b	
4. c	8. a	12. b	16. b	20. b	24. c	

TEST II. ANTONYMS

1. a	5. d	9. c	13. d	17. a	21. c	25. a
2. b	6. c	10. c	14. b	18. b	22. d	26. a
3. c	7. c	11. b	15. a	19. c	23. c	
4. c	8. a	12. d	16. c	20. d	24. d	

TEST III. CAUSE AND EFFECT

1. b	5. d	9. b	13. d	17. b	21. b	25. c
2. c	6. c	10. a	14. a	18. c	22. a	26. b
3. c	7. b	11. a	15. b	19. d	23. d	
4. c	8. b	12. b	16. a	20. c	24. d	

TEST IV. PART TO WHOLE

1. c	5. d	9. b	13. c	17. c	21. d	25. c
2. a	6. b	10. d	14. c	18. c	22. c	26. b
3. b	7. c	11. c	15. b	19. b	23. b	
4. c	8. b	12. b	16. d	20. d	24. c	

TEST V. PART TO PART

1. d	5. d	9. a	13. d	17. b	21. b	25. c
2. b	6. d	10. b	14. d	18. d	22. d	26. a
3. b	7. d	11. c	15. a	19. d	23. b	
4. b	8. d	12. b	16. c	20. b	24. c	

TEST VI. PURPOSE

1. b	5. d	9. c	13. d	17. b	21. d	25. b
2. a	6. a	10. b	14. c	18. b	22. d	26. c
3. d	7. a	11. b	15. d	19. a	23. c	
4. b	8. b	12. a	16. b	20. d	24. c	

TEST VII. ACTION TO OBJECT

1. c	5. b	9. b	13. b	17. b	21. b	25. c
2. b	6. d	10. a	14. a	18. c	22. a	26. a
3. a	7. a	11. d	15. d	19. d	23. c	
4. a	8. a	12. b	16. b	20. c	24. d	

TEST VIII. OBJECT TO ACTION

1. d	5. b	9. b	13. b	17. d	21. b	25. c
2. c	6. c	10. b	14. c	18. a	22. d	26. c
3. b	7. a	11. c	15. b	19. a	23. d	
4. b	8. c	12. b	16. b	20. b	24. b	

TEST IX. PLACE

1. d	5. b	9. c	13. d	17. d	21. d	25. a
2. d	6. d	10. b	14. d	18. a	22. b	26. a
3. a	7. c	11. c	15. b	19. b	23. a	
4. c	8. b	12. a	16. a	20. a	24. d	

TEST X. ASSOCIATION

1. a	5. c	9. b	13. a	17. b	21. c	25. c
2. d	6. a	10. d	14. a	18. d	22. b	26. a
3. a	7. a	11. c	15. b	19. d	23. c	
4. d	8. d	12. a	16. c	20. b	24. d	

TEST XI. SEQUENCE

1. a	5. b	9. c	13. c	17. c	21. c	25. b
2. a	6. d	10. b	14. b	18. a	22. c	26. d
3. b	7. b	11. c	15. b	19. d	23. b	
4. d	8. c	12. b	16. d	20. b	24. b	

TEST XII. CHARACTERISTIC

1. a	5. d	9. b	13. d	17. a	21. c	25. a
2. b	6. a	10. b	14. b	18. a	22. d	26. d
3. d	7. d	11. c	15. b	19. d	23. b	
4. d	8. c	12. d	16. b	20. c	24. d	

TEST XIII. DEGREE

1. a	5. d	9. b	13. b	17. c	21. b	25. b
2. b	6. b	10. b	14. d	18. b	22. a	26. b
3. d	7. d	11. b	15. a	19. a	23. c	
4. d	8. b	12. c	16. c	20. c	24. d	

TEXT XIV. GRAMMATICAL

1. b	5. b	9. a	13. c	17. b	21. b	25. a
2. c	6. a	10. b	14. c	18. b	22. d	26. d
3. c	7. b	11. d	15. b	19. c	23. b	
4. a	8. d	12. c	16. c	20. a	24. d	

Part Two
Five Sample Exams
With Explanatory Answers
for all Questions

ANSWER SHEET FOR
MILLER ANALOGIES SAMPLE TEST I

1 Ⓐ Ⓑ Ⓒ Ⓓ	26 Ⓐ Ⓑ Ⓒ Ⓓ	51 Ⓐ Ⓑ Ⓒ Ⓓ	76 Ⓐ Ⓑ Ⓒ Ⓓ
2 Ⓐ Ⓑ Ⓒ Ⓓ	27 Ⓐ Ⓑ Ⓒ Ⓓ	52 Ⓐ Ⓑ Ⓒ Ⓓ	77 Ⓐ Ⓑ Ⓒ Ⓓ
3 Ⓐ Ⓑ Ⓒ Ⓓ	28 Ⓐ Ⓑ Ⓒ Ⓓ	53 Ⓐ Ⓑ Ⓒ Ⓓ	78 Ⓐ Ⓑ Ⓒ Ⓓ
4 Ⓐ Ⓑ Ⓒ Ⓓ	29 Ⓐ Ⓑ Ⓒ Ⓓ	54 Ⓐ Ⓑ Ⓒ Ⓓ	79 Ⓐ Ⓑ Ⓒ Ⓓ
5 Ⓐ Ⓑ Ⓒ Ⓓ	30 Ⓐ Ⓑ Ⓒ Ⓓ	55 Ⓐ Ⓑ Ⓒ Ⓓ	80 Ⓐ Ⓑ Ⓒ Ⓓ
6 Ⓐ Ⓑ Ⓒ Ⓓ	31 Ⓐ Ⓑ Ⓒ Ⓓ	56 Ⓐ Ⓑ Ⓒ Ⓓ	81 Ⓐ Ⓑ Ⓒ Ⓓ
7 Ⓐ Ⓑ Ⓒ Ⓓ	32 Ⓐ Ⓑ Ⓒ Ⓓ	57 Ⓐ Ⓑ Ⓒ Ⓓ	82 Ⓐ Ⓑ Ⓒ Ⓓ
8 Ⓐ Ⓑ Ⓒ Ⓓ	33 Ⓐ Ⓑ Ⓒ Ⓓ	58 Ⓐ Ⓑ Ⓒ Ⓓ	83 Ⓐ Ⓑ Ⓒ Ⓓ
9 Ⓐ Ⓑ Ⓒ Ⓓ	34 Ⓐ Ⓑ Ⓒ Ⓓ	59 Ⓐ Ⓑ Ⓒ Ⓓ	84 Ⓐ Ⓑ Ⓒ Ⓓ
10 Ⓐ Ⓑ Ⓒ Ⓓ	35 Ⓐ Ⓑ Ⓒ Ⓓ	60 Ⓐ Ⓑ Ⓒ Ⓓ	85 Ⓐ Ⓑ Ⓒ Ⓓ
11 Ⓐ Ⓑ Ⓒ Ⓓ	36 Ⓐ Ⓑ Ⓒ Ⓓ	61 Ⓐ Ⓑ Ⓒ Ⓓ	86 Ⓐ Ⓑ Ⓒ Ⓓ
12 Ⓐ Ⓑ Ⓒ Ⓓ	37 Ⓐ Ⓑ Ⓒ Ⓓ	62 Ⓐ Ⓑ Ⓒ Ⓓ	87 Ⓐ Ⓑ Ⓒ Ⓓ
13 Ⓐ Ⓑ Ⓒ Ⓓ	38 Ⓐ Ⓑ Ⓒ Ⓓ	63 Ⓐ Ⓑ Ⓒ Ⓓ	88 Ⓐ Ⓑ Ⓒ Ⓓ
14 Ⓐ Ⓑ Ⓒ Ⓓ	39 Ⓐ Ⓑ Ⓒ Ⓓ	64 Ⓐ Ⓑ Ⓒ Ⓓ	89 Ⓐ Ⓑ Ⓒ Ⓓ
15 Ⓐ Ⓑ Ⓒ Ⓓ	40 Ⓐ Ⓑ Ⓒ Ⓓ	65 Ⓐ Ⓑ Ⓒ Ⓓ	90 Ⓐ Ⓑ Ⓒ Ⓓ
16 Ⓐ Ⓑ Ⓒ Ⓓ	41 Ⓐ Ⓑ Ⓒ Ⓓ	66 Ⓐ Ⓑ Ⓒ Ⓓ	91 Ⓐ Ⓑ Ⓒ Ⓓ
17 Ⓐ Ⓑ Ⓒ Ⓓ	42 Ⓐ Ⓑ Ⓒ Ⓓ	67 Ⓐ Ⓑ Ⓒ Ⓓ	92 Ⓐ Ⓑ Ⓒ Ⓓ
18 Ⓐ Ⓑ Ⓒ Ⓓ	43 Ⓐ Ⓑ Ⓒ Ⓓ	68 Ⓐ Ⓑ Ⓒ Ⓓ	93 Ⓐ Ⓑ Ⓒ Ⓓ
19 Ⓐ Ⓑ Ⓒ Ⓓ	44 Ⓐ Ⓑ Ⓒ Ⓓ	69 Ⓐ Ⓑ Ⓒ Ⓓ	94 Ⓐ Ⓑ Ⓒ Ⓓ
20 Ⓐ Ⓑ Ⓒ Ⓓ	45 Ⓐ Ⓑ Ⓒ Ⓓ	70 Ⓐ Ⓑ Ⓒ Ⓓ	95 Ⓐ Ⓑ Ⓒ Ⓓ
21 Ⓐ Ⓑ Ⓒ Ⓓ	46 Ⓐ Ⓑ Ⓒ Ⓓ	71 Ⓐ Ⓑ Ⓒ Ⓓ	96 Ⓐ Ⓑ Ⓒ Ⓓ
22 Ⓐ Ⓑ Ⓒ Ⓓ	47 Ⓐ Ⓑ Ⓒ Ⓓ	72 Ⓐ Ⓑ Ⓒ Ⓓ	97 Ⓐ Ⓑ Ⓒ Ⓓ
23 Ⓐ Ⓑ Ⓒ Ⓓ	48 Ⓐ Ⓑ Ⓒ Ⓓ	73 Ⓐ Ⓑ Ⓒ Ⓓ	98 Ⓐ Ⓑ Ⓒ Ⓓ
24 Ⓐ Ⓑ Ⓒ Ⓓ	49 Ⓐ Ⓑ Ⓒ Ⓓ	74 Ⓐ Ⓑ Ⓒ Ⓓ	99 Ⓐ Ⓑ Ⓒ Ⓓ
25 Ⓐ Ⓑ Ⓒ Ⓓ	50 Ⓐ Ⓑ Ⓒ Ⓓ	75 Ⓐ Ⓑ Ⓒ Ⓓ	100 Ⓐ Ⓑ Ⓒ Ⓓ

MILLER ANALOGIES SAMPLE TEST I

Directions: Each of these test questions consists of three CAPI-TALIZED words and four lettered words enclosed in parentheses. Two of the capitalized words are related in some way. Find the two related words and establish the nature of the relationship. Then study the four words lettered a, b, c and d. Select the one lettered word which is related to the remaining capitalized word in the same way that the first two capitalized words are related. Mark the Answer Sheet for the letter preceding the word you select.

1. BALMY : MILD :: FAITHFUL : (a. explosive, b. docile, c. talkative, d. staunch)

2. BOLD : TIMID :: SQUANDER : (a. disperse, b. retrench, c. query, d. extinguish)

3. SEA : (a. fish, b. ocean, c. island, d. net) :: LAND : LAKE

4. BOTTLE : BRITTLE :: TIRE : (a. elastic, b. scarce, c. rubber, d. spheroid)

5. DIAMETER : RADIUS :: (a. 3, b. 8, c. 5, d. 6) : 4

6. GLABROUS : HIRSUTE :: FACTITIOUS : (a. authentic, b. fictional, c. fluent, d. replete)

7. PARANOIA : SCHIZOPHRENIA :: MEGALOMANIA : (a. melancholia, b. carcinoma, c. hepatitis, d. glaucoma)

8. (a. sales, b. investment, c. management, d. interest) : PROFIT :: LABOR : WAGES

9. HOBO : (a. knapsack, b. vagrant, c. park, d. slum) :: TRAVELER : TRUNK

10. DENIGRATE : DEFAMER :: MEDIATE : (a. mathematician, b. arbitrator, c. employer, d. laborer)

11. INDUCTILE : INDOMITABLE :: SEJANT : (a. reticent, b. remarkable, c. sojourning, d. sitting)

12. CORNET : OBOE :: (a. cello, b. drum, c. harpsichord, d. xylophone) : GUITAR

13. JANUARY : JANUS :: WEDNESDAY : (a. Thor, b. Apollo, c. Odin, d. Diana)

14. HORSE : (a. equestrian, b. hoofed, c. cabriolet, d. herbivorous) :: TIGER : CARNIVOROUS

15. GOOD : BETTER :: (a. terrible, b. worse, c. improvement, d. bad) : WORST

16. CLAN : FEUD :: NATION : (a. war, b. politics, c. armaments, d. retaliation)

17. ABUNDANCE : DEARTH :: ABROGATE : (a. deny, b. establish, c. abstain, d. absolve)

18. ONOMATOPOEIA : METAPHOR :: SOUND : (a. hiss, b. rhyme, c. saying, d. comparison)

19. SACRAMENTO : HELENA :: ALBANY : (a. New York, b. Little Rock, c. Houston, d. San Francisco)

20. (a. scan, b. feel, c. dear, d. seen) : READ :: REAP : PEAR

21. CAUTIOUS : CIRCUMSPECT :: PRECIPITOUS : (a. premonitory, b. profound, c. stealthy, d. steep)

22. SEISMOGRAPH : GEOLOGY :: ELECTROENCEPHALOGRAPH : (a. bacteriology, b. biology, c. neurology, d. cardiology)

23. ACUTE : CHRONIC :: VENERATE : (a. revere, b. actuate, c. flout, d. repent)

24. (a. toad, b. lion, c. shark, d. alligator) : TURTLE :: TIGER : MAN

25. INSTINCT : PLAN :: UNCONSCIOUS : (a. involuntary, b. intentional, c. spontaneous, d. imaginary)

26. INDIA : (a. Sri Lanka, b. Greece, c. Afghanistan, d. Pakistan) : : ITALY : SWITZERLAND

27. SWIM : SWAM :: BURST : (a. busted, b. bursted, c. burst, d. bust)

28. RAISIN : GRAPE :: PRUNE : (a. apricot, b. currant, c. plum, d. berry)

29. GRAM : OUNCE :: LITER : (a. deciliter, b. quart, c. kilogram, d. pound)

30. PESTLE : PHARMACIST :: STETHOSCOPE : (a. teacher, b. author, c. physician, d. doctor)

31. LIMPID : LUCID :: TURBID : (a. torpid, b. muddy, c. truculent, d. serene)

32. PEACH : (a. tomato, b. banana, c. cabbage, d. coconut) :: GRAPE : PLUM

33. .02 : .0004 :: .001 : (a. 000001, b. .0001, c. .0002, d. .000002)

34. SADNESS : FAILURE :: PAIN : (a. medication, b. palliation, c. pleasure, d. injury)

35. AMELIA EARHART : AVIATION :: NELLIE BLY : (a. medicine, b. journalism, c. law, d. prohibition)

36. ROMAN : MANOR :: (a. cleric, b. names, c. patrimony, d. estates) : MANSE

37. LACONIC : REDUNDANT :: FLACCID : (a. succinct, b. resilient, c. flimsy, d. swollen)

38. PNEUMATICS : (a. medicine, b. disease, c. physics, d. cars) :: ESKER : GEOLOGY

39. NECKLACE : ADORNMENT :: MEDAL : (a. jewel, b. metal, c. decoration, d. bronze)

40. RIVER : STREAM :: MOUNTAIN : (a. cliff, b. hill, c. canyon, d. peak)

41. HECKLE : NEEDLE :: (a. stock, b. deplete, c. book, d. stylus) : REPLENISH

42. (a. guerrilla, b. terrorist, c. quash, d. mediate) : REBELLION :: NEGOTIATE : TREATY

43. BOTANIST : PLANTS :: GEOLOGIST : (a. trees, b. rocks, c. geography, d. gems)

44. CAT : FELINE :: OX : (a. equine, b. saturnine, c. bovine, d. canine)

45. WOLF : (a. wool, b. sheep, c. ewe, d. ram) :: DOG : CAT

46. (a. 5/16, b. 3/8, c. 2/6, d. 5/12) : 9/24 :: 4/11 : 12/33

47. FISHES : BIRDS :: (a. horses, b. cattle, c. wheat, d. mosses) : CEREALS

48. OFFICE : DESK :: ROOM : (a. space, b. wallpaper, c. apartment, d. furniture)

49. BRASS : COPPER :: PEWTER : (a. lead, b. zinc, c. silver, d. bronze)

50. COWCATCHER : LOCOMOTIVE :: (a. coda, b. climax, c. epilogue, d. finale) : DENOUEMENT

51. PARIAH : OUTCAST :: ARCHON : (a. archivist, b. magistrate, c. martinet, d. constable)

52. SAMSON : HAIR :: ACHILLES : (a. heel, b. spear, c. victory, d. war)

53. LANCET : CUT :: CHAMOIS : (a. polish, b. pliant, c. smooth, d. sheep)

54. (a. utter, b. elapse, c. exude, d. time) : EMIT :: STEP : PETS

55. SAFE : COMBINATION :: NECKLACE : (a. torque, b. bangle, c. circlet, d. clasp)

56. EXPERIMENT : (a. science, b. elucidation, c. hypothesis, d. investigation) :: EXAMINATION : ACHIEVEMENT

57. BOY : MAN :: BULLET : (a. gun, b. artillery shell, c. holster, d. trigger)

58. ENERVATE : (a. eradicate, b. invigorate, c. disconcert, d. propagate) :: MALICE : BENEVOLENCE

59. EVIDENCE : CONVICTION :: (a. oxygen, b. carbon dioxide, c. heat, d. light) : COMBUSTION

60. EDIFICATION : AWARENESS :: EXACERBATION : (a. soreness, b. excitement, c. reduction, d. deliberation)

61. NEWTON : COPERNICUS :: SHAKESPEARE : (a. Fielding, b. Jonson, c. Dickens, d. Pope)

62. SAINT AUGUSTINE : (a. Florida, b. Virginia, c. France, d. Spain) :: JAMESTOWN : ENGLAND

63. SNOW : DRIFT :: (a. hill, b. rain, c. sand, d. desert) : DUNE

64. CATAMARAN : RAFT :: TERMAGANT : (a. grisette, b. spinnaker, c. spinster, d. shrew)

65. 3^2 : 2^3 :: 9 : (a. 1, b. 6, c. 4, d. 8)

66 FICTION : NOVELIST :: FACTS : (a. legend, b. story, c. historian, d. research)

67. HARVARD : YALE :: SMITH : (a. Princeton, b. Purdue, c. Columbia, d. Dartmouth)

68. CAT : WOLF :: (a. lion, b. dog, c. man, d. tiger) : DUCK

69. WHO : WHOM :: I : (a. we, b. me, c. whose, d. mine)

70. (a. obsequious, b. obstreperous, c. complacent, d. contumelious) : SYCOPHANT :: CONTUMACIOUS : RENEGADE

71. DOWSER : ROD :: GEOMANCER : (a. stones, b. maps, c. plants, d. configurations)

72. RAIN : (a. water, b. cold, c. moisture, d. snow) :: BOIL : SIMMER

73. (a. loss, b. victory, c. game, d. team) : WIN :: MEDICINE : CURE

74. FLINT : (a. stone, b. fire, c. clap, d. flit) :: FLIRT : FLIGHT

75. ACID : ALKALI :: 6 : (a. 1, b. 4, c. 7, d. 8)

76. PEDESTAL : (a. column, b. sculpture, c. chandelier, d. stone) :: STALAGMITE : STALACTITE

77. BONA FIDE : IN TOTO :: CARTE BLANCHE : (a. eureka, b. status quo, c. avant-garde, d. ersatz)

78. SEA : COAST :: RIVER : (a. inlet, b. delta, c. stream, d. bank)

79. AMOUNT : NUMBER :: (a. lessen, b. augment, c. less, d. enumerate) : FEWER

80. VOLUME : CUBIC METER :: (a. area, b. length, c. capacity, d. mass) : LITER

81. (a. refrain, b. precede, c. sustain, d. foray) : FORBEAR :: ADUMBRATE : FORESHADOW

82. CHAMPION : CAUSE :: (a. signature, b. introduction, c. draft, d. ink) : LETTER

83. SHADOWS : SUN :: CLOUDS : (a. water, b. dark, c. rain, d. thunder)

84. WINTER : SUMMER :: BOSTON : (a. Miami, b. Madrid, c. São Paulo, d. San Diego)

85. CIRCLE : SPHERE :: (a. ice, b. angle, c. oval, d. square) : CUBE

86. KINETIC : MOTION :: PISCATORIAL : (a. pizza, b. painting, c. fish, d. picturesque)

87. RESPIRATION : CO_2 :: (a. hydrolysis, b. transpiration, c. oxidation, d. photosynthesis) : O_2

88. SAND : GLASS :: CLAY : (a. stone, b. hay, c. brick, d. dirt)

89. LOUISIANA PURCHASE : (a. Mexico, b. Spain, c. Great Britain, d. France) :: ALASKA : RUSSIA

90. X : M :: (a. V, b. X, c. L, d. I) : C

91. PUCCINI : OPERA :: (a. Pavlova, b. Verdi, c. Giselle, d. Balanchine) : BALLET

92. POLTROON : TERROR :: PARANOIAC : (a. courage, b. shyness, c. persecution, d. paralysis)

93. DOOR : BOLT :: LETTER : (a. envelope, b. mail, c. seal, d. write)

94. AUTHOR : (a. royalties, b. charges, c. fees, d. contributions) :: AGENT : COMMISSIONS

95. LAY : LIES :: ATE : (a. eaten, b. eats, c. eating, d. eat)

96. DINNER : DINE :: THINNER : (a. think, b. thine, c. tine, d. mine)

97. ORAL : AURAL :: SPEAK : (a. smell, b. see, c. sense, d. hear)

98. ACID : (a. $NaHCO_3$, b. H_2SO_4, c. NaCl, d. NaOH) :: ENZYME : AMYLASE

99. (a. sow, b. doe, c. vixen, d. bitch) : FOX :: DAM : SIRE

100. SALIVA : MOUTH :: OIL : (a. friction, b. comb, c. motor, d. cogwheel)

ANSWER KEY FOR MILLER ANALOGIES SAMPLE TEST I

1.	d	21.	d	41.	a	61.	b	81.	a
2.	b	22.	c	42.	c	62.	d	82.	c
3.	c	23.	c	43.	b	63.	c	83.	a
4.	a	24.	d	44.	c	64.	d	84.	c
5.	b	25.	b	45.	b	65.	d	85.	d
6.	a	26.	d	46.	b	66.	c	86.	c
7.	a	27.	c	47.	d	67.	d	87.	d
8.	a	28.	c	48.	d	68.	c	88.	c
9.	a	29.	b	49.	a	69.	b	89.	d
10.	b	30.	c	50.	b	70.	a	90.	d
11.	d	31.	b	51.	b	71.	d	91.	d
12.	a	32.	a	52.	a	72.	d	92.	c
13.	c	33.	a	53.	b a	73.	c	93.	c
14.	d	34.	d	54.	d	74.	d	94.	a
15.	b	35.	b	55.	d	75.	d	95.	b
16.	a	36.	b	56.	c	76.	c	96.	b
17.	b	37.	b	57.	b	77.	c	97.	d
18.	d	38.	c	58.	b	78.	d	98.	b
19.	b	39.	c	59.	a	79.	c	99.	c
20.	c	40.	b	60.	a	80.	c	100.	c

EXPLANATORY ANSWERS FOR
MILLER ANALOGIES SAMPLE TEST I

1. (d) BALMY and MILD are synonyms; therefore, the task is to look for a synonym for FAITHFUL, which in this case is STAUNCH.

2. (b) BOLD and TIMID are related as antonyms. SQUANDER, meaning to spend extravagantly, is the opposite of RETRENCH, meaning to curtail or economize.

3. (c) LAND and LAKE are related geographically in the same way as SEA and ISLAND; for as land surrounds a lake so does sea surround an island.

4. (a) A specific characteristic of a BOTTLE is that it is BRITTLE. Similarly, a specific characteristic of a TIRE is that it is ELASTIC.

5. (b) This is a mathematical relationship. A DIAMETER is twice the length of a RADIUS in a given circle; therefore, the missing term must be a number that is twice as great as 4. That, of course, is 8.

6. (a) GLABROUS (hairless) and HIRSUTE (hairy) are antonyms. The only antonym for FACTITIOUS (artificial) is AUTHENTIC.

7. (a) Every term in this analogy is a form of illness. PARANOIA, a psychosis characterized by delusions of persecution, and SCHIZO-PHRENIA, a psychosis characterized by disintegration of the personality, are related by the fact that each is a form of mental illness. MEGALO-MANIA, a psychosis characterized by infantile feelings of personal omnipotence, is also a form of mental illness. Therefore, the missing term must be MELANCHOLIA, a psychosis characterized by extreme depression, because this is the only alternative that names a mental, rather than a physical, illness.

8. (a) LABOR is associated with WAGES in the same way that MANAGE-MENT is associated with PROFIT. In both cases the association is of people working for a reward. Sales, investment and interest may each be said to yield a profit, but these do not parallel the relationship of people to their reward as established by the given word pair.

9. (a) This is an analogy of purpose. A TRAVELER uses a TRUNK in the same way that a HOBO uses a KNAPSACK.

10. (b) The relationship is one of action to object. DENIGRATE (to belittle or to malign) is the action taken by the DEFAMER (one who injures by giving misleading or false reports) in the same way that MEDIATE (to act as an intermediary agent) is the action taken by the ARBITRATOR (one chosen to settle differences between parties in dispute).

11. (d) INDUCTILE and INDOMITABLE are synonyms meaning unyielding. The only synonym offered for SEJANT is SITTING.

12. (a) This is a part-to-part analogy. CORNET and OBOE are each part of the larger category of wind instruments in the same way that GUITAR and CELLO are each part of the larger category of string instruments. Harpsichord, too, belongs to the category of string instruments; however, because it has internal, rather than external, strings, it is not as closely related to guitar as is cello.

13. (c) JANUARY was named for JANUS, the guardian deity of gates in Roman mythology, as WEDNESDAY was named for ODIN, chief of the Scandinavian gods. The Anglo-Saxon version of Odin was Woden; hence Woden's Day became Wednesday.

14. (b) This is a characteristic relationship. A specific characteristic of a TIGER is that it is CARNIVOROUS (meat-eating) as a specific characteristic of a HORSE is that it is HERBIVOROUS (plant-eating).

15. (b) This is an analogy of degree. Adjectives such as good and bad have three degrees of comparison: positive, comparative and superlative. In this question, GOOD, which is the positive degree, is smaller than BETTER, the comparative degree, to the same extent as WORSE, the comparative,

is smaller than WORST, the superlative degree.

16. (a) The relationship is one of object to action. Just as a CLAN may become involved in a FEUD, so may a NATION become involved in a WAR.

17. (b) ABUNDANCE and DEARTH are antonyms. The opposite of ABROGATE (to nullify or cancel) is ESTABLISH.

18. (d) ONOMATOPOEIA (a word whose sound suggests its'sense) is a figure of speech that makes a SOUND relationship. METAPHOR (an implied comparison between unlike things) is a figure of speech that makes a COMPARISON.

19. (b) SACRAMENTO and HELENA are related because each is a capital city. Sacramento is the capital of California and Helena the capital of Montana. Since ALBANY is also a state capital, it must be paired with LITTLE ROCK, the capital of Arkansas, to complete the analogy.

20. (c) This is a non-semantic analogy. Transposing the first and last letters of REAP forms the word PEAR just as transposing the first and last letters of READ forms the word DEAR.

21. (d) CAUTIOUS and CIRCUMSPECT are related as synonyms. The only synonym offered for PRECIPITOUS is STEEP.

22. (c) This is an analogy of association. A SEISMOGRAPH, an instrument for recording vibrations within the earth, is used in GEOLOGY (the study of the earth) as an ELECTROENCEPHALOGRAPH, an instrument for recording brain waves, is used in NEUROLOGY (the scientific study of the nervous system).

23. (c) ACUTE and CHRONIC are related as antonyms. Acute means having a sudden onset, sharp rise and short course; chronic means marked by long duration or frequent recurrence. VENERATE, which means to honor, must therefore be paired with its opposite, FLOUT, meaning to scoff or to treat with contemptuous disregard, in order to complete the analogy.

24. (d) This is a part to part analogy. TIGER and MAN are each part of the larger category of mammals. TURTLE, which is part of the larger category of reptiles, must therefore be paired with ALLIGATOR, the only reptile among the answer choices.

25. (b) An INSTINCT is an unreasoned or UNCONSCIOUS response to a stimulus. A PLAN is a reasoned or INTENTIONAL response to a stimulus.

26. (d) The relationship between ITALY and SWITZERLAND is that they share a common border, as do INDIA and PAKISTAN.

27. (c) The grammatical relationship between SWIM and SWAM is one of present tense to past tense; therefore, the task is to find the past tense of BURST, which is also BURST.

28. (c) The relationship is one of origin. A RAISIN is a dried GRAPE just as a PRUNE is a dried PLUM.

29. (b) The relationship between GRAM and OUNCE is one of metric to customary measures of weight. Since a LITER is a metric measure of capacity, it must be paired with a customary measure of capacity, which is QUART.

30. (c) This is an analogy of tool to its user. A PESTLE is used by a PHARMACIST in the performance of his work as a STETHOSCOPE is used by a PHYSICIAN in the performance of his work. Choice (d) is incorrect because it is not as specific as (c); not all doctors are physicians.

31. (b) LIMPID and LUCID are synonyms meaning clear. A synonym for TURBID is MUDDY.

32. (a) The PEACH, TOMATO, GRAPE and PLUM are all juicy fruits that are grown in temperate climates.

33. (a) $(.02)^2 = .0004$; $(.001)^2 = .000001$.

34. (d) The relationship of the given word pair is one of cause and effect. SADNESS may be caused by FAILURE in the same way that PAIN may be caused by an INJURY.

35. (b) This is an analogy of the association of famous women to the field in which they pioneered. AMELIA EARHART achieved fame as one of the first women in AVIATION; NELLIE BLY, as one of the first women in JOURNALISM.

36. (b) ROMAN and MANOR are anagrams. So, too, are NAMES and MANSE.

37. (b) LACONIC (concise) and REDUNDANT (excessively wordy) are antonyms. Among the answer choices, the only antonym for FLACCID (flabby or limp) is RESILIENT (flexible).

38. (c) An ESKER (a ridge formed by a glacial stream) is part of the field of GEOLOGY as PNEUMATICS (the use of gas or air pressure) is part of the field of PHYSICS.

39. (c) A NECKLACE is used for ADORNMENT as a MEDAL is used for DECORATION.

40. (b) This is an analogy of degree. A RIVER is larger than a STREAM as a MOUNTAIN is larger than a HILL.

41. (a) HECKLE and NEEDLE are synonyms meaning to harass or badger. The only synonym offered for REPLENISH is STOCK.

42. (c) The relationship of the given word pair is object to action. One may NEGOTIATE (bring about by mutual agreement) a TREATY just as one may QUASH (crush) a REBELLION.

43. (b) The first word pair is related by the association of a scientist to his study. Of the choices offered, only the study of ROCKS is related to the GEOLOGIST as the study of PLANTS is related to the BOTANIST.

44. (c) FELINE means of or relating to the CAT family as BOVINE means of or relating to the OX or cow.

45. (b) The DOG is the traditional enemy of the CAT as the WOLF is the traditional enemy of SHEEP. Ewe (a female sheep) and ram (a male sheep) are incorrect because they are too specific. The relationship established by the given word pair calls for a general family name.

46. (b) Dividing numerator and denominator by 3, 12/33 can be reduced to 4/11. Similarly, dividing numerator and denominator by 3, 9/24 can be reduced to 3/8.

47. (d) This is an analogy of sequence. On the evolutionary scale, FISHES appeared long before BIRDS in the animal world; MOSSES, long before CEREALS in the plant world.

48. (d) The relationship between the terms of the given word pair is one of place. An OFFICE is likely to contain a DESK just as a ROOM is likely to contain FURNITURE.

49. (a) BRASS is an alloy consisting essentially of COPPER and zinc. PEWTER is an alloy consisting of tin and LEAD.

50. (b) A COWCATCHER immediately precedes a LOCOMOTIVE as a CLIMAX (the point of highest dramatic tension) immediately precedes the DENOUEMENT (the unraveling or outcome of a sequence of events) in a story or a play.

51. (b) PARIAH and OUTCAST are synonyms. The only synonym offered for ARCHON is MAGISTRATE.

52. (a) SAMSON's weak spot was his HAIR just as ACHILLES' weak spot was his HEEL.

53. (b) This is an analogy of purpose. A LANCET is a sharp surgical instrument used to cut; a CHAMOIS is a soft, pliant leather prepared from the skin of the chamois or from sheepskin used to polish.

54. (d) This is a non-semantic analogy. TIME spelled backwards is EMIT as STEP spelled backwards is PETS.

55. (d) A SAFE is opened by a COMBINATION; a NECKLACE by a CLASP.

56. (c) An EXPERIMENT tests a HYPOTHESIS as an EXAMINATION tests ACHIEVEMENT.

57. (b) BOY and MAN are each part of the larger category of human males. BULLET and ARTILLERY SHELL are each part of the larger category of missile weapons.

58. (b) MALICE and BENEVOLENCE are antonyms. The only antonym offered for ENERVATE is INVIGORATE.

59. (a) EVIDENCE is necessary for CONVICTION in the judicial process just as OXYGEN is necessary for the chemical process of COMBUSTION.

60. (a) The relationship of the given word pair is one of cause and effect since EDIFICATION (enlightenment) results in AWARENESS. Similarly, EXACERBATION (aggravation) results in SORENESS.

61. (b) NEWTON and COPERNICUS are noted for their contributions to the field of science. SHAKESPEARE and JONSON are well-known for their drama and poetry. Notice that each of the alternatives names a figure from the field of literature; therefore, it is necessary to narrow the relationship to a particular area of literature in order to answer this question correctly.

62. (d) SAINT AUGUSTINE was the first permanent settlement in the United States founded by SPAIN. JAMESTOWN was the first permanent settlement to be founded by ENGLAND.

63. (c) When blown by the wind, SNOW forms a DRIFT and SAND forms a DUNE.

64. (d) CATAMARAN and RAFT are synonyms as are TERMAGANT and SHREW.

65. (d) $3^2 = 3 \times 3 = 9$
$2^3 = 2 \times 2 \times 2 = 8$

66. (c) FICTION is the province of the NOVELIST as FACTS are the province of the HISTORIAN.

67. (d) The relationship between the terms of the given word pair is one of place. HARVARD and YALE are both located in New England as are SMITH and DARTMOUTH.

68. (c) CAT and WOLF are related in that they are each members of the larger category of four-legged creatures. DUCK, which is a two-legged creature, must therefore be paired with the only other two-legged creature, which is MAN.

69. (b) This is a grammatical analogy. WHO is nominative and WHOM is objective. Likewise, I is nominative and ME is objective.

70. (a) The relationship between the words of the given pair is one of characteristic. CONTUMACIOUS (an adjective meaning rebellious) describes a RENEGADE (a noun meaning one who rejects lawful or conventional behavior). Similarly OBSEQUIOUS (an adjective meaning subservient) describes a SYCOPHANT (a noun meaning servile flatterer or parasite).

71. (d) A DOWSER divines the presence of water or minerals by means of a ROD as a GEOMANCER divines by means of geographical features or CONFIGURATIONS.

72. (d) This is an analogy of degree. As the temperature falls, RAIN changes to SNOW and a BOIL is reduced to a SIMMER.

73. (c) The object of a GAME is to WIN as the object of MEDICINE is to CURE. The relationship is one of object to action.

74. (d) In this non-semantic analogy, the only relationship that exists among FLIRT, FLIGHT and FLINT is that each word contains the letters F, L, I and T. Of the answer choices only (d) FLIT satisfies the requirements of this relationship.

75. (d) Acidity and alkalinity are expressed on a pH scale whose values run from 0 to 14, with 7 representing neutrality. Numbers less than 7 indicate increasing acidity and numbers greater than 7 represent increasing alkalinity. Therefore, ACID : ALKALI :: 6 (a pH indicating mild acidity) : 8 (a pH indicating mild alkalinity).

76. (c) Stalagmites and stalactites are deposits of calcium carbonate formed by the dripping of calcareous water in a cave. A STALAGMITE grows up from the floor of the cave, while a STALACTITE hangs down from the ceiling of the cave. Similarly, a PEDESTAL is an architectural support or base that raises something up from the ground and a CHANDELIER is a lighting fixture that hangs down from the ceiling.

77. (c) BONA FIDE (meaning in good faith) and IN TOTO (meaning in full) are Latin words which have been borrowed intact for use in English. AVANT-GARDE (meaning pioneer) and CARTE BLANCHE (meaning blanket permission) are French words which have been borrowed intact for use in English. Eureka is borrowed from the Greek; status quo, from Latin; and ersatz, from German.

78. (d) This is an analogy of place. The land bordering the SEA is the COAST as the land bordering a RIVER is a BANK.

79. (c) In this grammatical analogy, AMOUNT refers to quantity or bulk while NUMBER refers to items that can be counted one by one. Similarly, LESS refers to quantity and FEWER to items that can be counted.

80. (c) The relationship expressed by the given word pair is one of measurement. VOLUME may be measured in CUBIC METER as CAPACITY may be measured in LITER.

81. (a) ADUMBRATE and FORESHADOW are synonyms. The only synonym offered for FORBEAR (meaning to hold back or abstain) is REFRAIN.

82. (c) This is an analogy of action to object. One may CHAMPION a CAUSE as one may DRAFT a LETTER.

83. (a) SUN is necessary to the formation of SHADOWS as WATER is necessary to the formation of CLOUDS.

84. (c) When it is WINTER in BOSTON, it is SUMMER in SÃO PAULO since the seasons are reversed in the northern and southern hemispheres.

85. (d) A CIRCLE is a plane figure; a SPHERE, the corresponding solid figure. A SQUARE is a plane figure and a CUBE the corresponding solid figure.

86. (c) KINETIC is an adjective meaning of or relating to MOTION as PISCATORIAL is an adjective meaning of or relating to FISH.

87. (d) During the process of RESPIRATION, living things take in oxygen and give off CO_2 and water. During the process of PHOTOSYNTHESIS, green plants take in carbon dioxide and water and give off O_2.

88. (c) The relationship existing between the terms of the given word pair is one of purpose since SAND is used to make GLASS. Similarly, CLAY is used to make BRICK.

89. (d) ALASKA was purchased from RUSSIA (in 1867) as the area known as the LOUISIANA PURCHASE was purchased from FRANCE (in 1803).

90. (d) The relationship between the Roman numerals X (10) and M (1000) is 1 to 100. The same relationship exists between the Roman numerals I (1) and C (100).

91. (d) PUCCINI creates OPERAS as BALANCHINE creates BALLETS. Although Pavlova was a famous ballerina and Giselle is the name of a well-known ballet, only Balanchine (as a choreographer) stands in the same relationship to the ballet as Puccini (as a composer) stands in relationship to opera.

92. (c) A characteristic of a POLTROON (coward) is a feeling of TERROR as a characteristic of a PARANOIAC is a feeling of PERSECUTION.

93. (c) The relationship between the terms of the given word pair is one of object to action. However, three of the choices offered are actions one may take on the object letter. Therefore, it is necessary to narrow the relationship to the specific action of closing or securing. A DOOR is secured by a BOLT and a LETTER is secured by a SEAL.

94. (a) The relationship is one of an individual to his means of payment. An AGENT receives COMMISSIONS (a percentage of the total fees paid) for his part in a business transaction. An AUTHOR receives ROYALTIES (a percentage of the total payment made for a work) for his part in creating the work sold.

95. (b) In this grammatical analogy, LAY, the past tense of the verb to lie, is paired with LIES, the third person, singular, present tense of the same verb. Therefore, ATE, the past tense of the verb to eat, must be paired with EATS, the third person, singular, present tense of the same verb.

96. (b) This is a non-semantic analogy. Dropping the letters N and R from DINNER leaves DINE. Dropping the letters N and R from THINNER leaves THINE.

97. (d) ORAL means uttered by the mouth or spoken. AURAL means of or relating to the ear or to the sense of hearing. Therefore, ORAL describes SPEAK as AURAL describes HEAR.

98. (b) The formula for a specific ACID is H_2SO_4 (sulphuric acid). The name for a specific ENZYME is AMYLASE.

99. (c) This analogy is one of female to male. VIXEN is a female animal and FOX is her male counterpart. DAM is a female animal parent and SIRE is the male counterpart.

100. (c) A characteristic of SALIVA is that it lubricates the MOUTH. A characteristic of OIL is that it lubricates a MOTOR.

ANSWER SHEET FOR
MILLER ANALOGIES SAMPLE TEST II

1 Ⓐ Ⓑ Ⓒ Ⓓ	26 Ⓐ Ⓑ Ⓒ Ⓓ	51 Ⓐ Ⓑ Ⓒ Ⓓ	76 Ⓐ Ⓑ Ⓒ Ⓓ
2 Ⓐ Ⓑ Ⓒ Ⓓ	27 Ⓐ Ⓑ Ⓒ Ⓓ	52 Ⓐ Ⓑ Ⓒ Ⓓ	77 Ⓐ Ⓑ Ⓒ Ⓓ
3 Ⓐ Ⓑ Ⓒ Ⓓ	28 Ⓐ Ⓑ Ⓒ Ⓓ	53 Ⓐ Ⓑ Ⓒ Ⓓ	78 Ⓐ Ⓑ Ⓒ Ⓓ
4 Ⓐ Ⓑ Ⓒ Ⓓ	29 Ⓐ Ⓑ Ⓒ Ⓓ	54 Ⓐ Ⓑ Ⓒ Ⓓ	79 Ⓐ Ⓑ Ⓒ Ⓓ
5 Ⓐ Ⓑ Ⓒ Ⓓ	30 Ⓐ Ⓑ Ⓒ Ⓓ	55 Ⓐ Ⓑ Ⓒ Ⓓ	80 Ⓐ Ⓑ Ⓒ Ⓓ
6 Ⓐ Ⓑ Ⓒ Ⓓ	31 Ⓐ Ⓑ Ⓒ Ⓓ	56 Ⓐ Ⓑ Ⓒ Ⓓ	81 Ⓐ Ⓑ Ⓒ Ⓓ
7 Ⓐ Ⓑ Ⓒ Ⓓ	32 Ⓐ Ⓑ Ⓒ Ⓓ	57 Ⓐ Ⓑ Ⓒ Ⓓ	82 Ⓐ Ⓑ Ⓒ Ⓓ
8 Ⓐ Ⓑ Ⓒ Ⓓ	33 Ⓐ Ⓑ Ⓒ Ⓓ	58 Ⓐ Ⓑ Ⓒ Ⓓ	83 Ⓐ Ⓑ Ⓒ Ⓓ
9 Ⓐ Ⓑ Ⓒ Ⓓ	34 Ⓐ Ⓑ Ⓒ Ⓓ	59 Ⓐ Ⓑ Ⓒ Ⓓ	84 Ⓐ Ⓑ Ⓒ Ⓓ
10 Ⓐ Ⓑ Ⓒ Ⓓ	35 Ⓐ Ⓑ Ⓒ Ⓓ	60 Ⓐ Ⓑ Ⓒ Ⓓ	85 Ⓐ Ⓑ Ⓒ Ⓓ
11 Ⓐ Ⓑ Ⓒ Ⓓ	36 Ⓐ Ⓑ Ⓒ Ⓓ	61 Ⓐ Ⓑ Ⓒ Ⓓ	86 Ⓐ Ⓑ Ⓒ Ⓓ
12 Ⓐ Ⓑ Ⓒ Ⓓ	37 Ⓐ Ⓑ Ⓒ Ⓓ	62 Ⓐ Ⓑ Ⓒ Ⓓ	87 Ⓐ Ⓑ Ⓒ Ⓓ
13 Ⓐ Ⓑ Ⓒ Ⓓ	38 Ⓐ Ⓑ Ⓒ Ⓓ	63 Ⓐ Ⓑ Ⓒ Ⓓ	88 Ⓐ Ⓑ Ⓒ Ⓓ
14 Ⓐ Ⓑ Ⓒ Ⓓ	39 Ⓐ Ⓑ Ⓒ Ⓓ	64 Ⓐ Ⓑ Ⓒ Ⓓ	89 Ⓐ Ⓑ Ⓒ Ⓓ
15 Ⓐ Ⓑ Ⓒ Ⓓ	40 Ⓐ Ⓑ Ⓒ Ⓓ	65 Ⓐ Ⓑ Ⓒ Ⓓ	90 Ⓐ Ⓑ Ⓒ Ⓓ
16 Ⓐ Ⓑ Ⓒ Ⓓ	41 Ⓐ Ⓑ Ⓒ Ⓓ	66 Ⓐ Ⓑ Ⓒ Ⓓ	91 Ⓐ Ⓑ Ⓒ Ⓓ
17 Ⓐ Ⓑ Ⓒ Ⓓ	42 Ⓐ Ⓑ Ⓒ Ⓓ	67 Ⓐ Ⓑ Ⓒ Ⓓ	92 Ⓐ Ⓑ Ⓒ Ⓓ
18 Ⓐ Ⓑ Ⓒ Ⓓ	43 Ⓐ Ⓑ Ⓒ Ⓓ	68 Ⓐ Ⓑ Ⓒ Ⓓ	93 Ⓐ Ⓑ Ⓒ Ⓓ
19 Ⓐ Ⓑ Ⓒ Ⓓ	44 Ⓐ Ⓑ Ⓒ Ⓓ	69 Ⓐ Ⓑ Ⓒ Ⓓ	94 Ⓐ Ⓑ Ⓒ Ⓓ
20 Ⓐ Ⓑ Ⓒ Ⓓ	45 Ⓐ Ⓑ Ⓒ Ⓓ	70 Ⓐ Ⓑ Ⓒ Ⓓ	95 Ⓐ Ⓑ Ⓒ Ⓓ
21 Ⓐ Ⓑ Ⓒ Ⓓ	46 Ⓐ Ⓑ Ⓒ Ⓓ	71 Ⓐ Ⓑ Ⓒ Ⓓ	96 Ⓐ Ⓑ Ⓒ Ⓓ
22 Ⓐ Ⓑ Ⓒ Ⓓ	47 Ⓐ Ⓑ Ⓒ Ⓓ	72 Ⓐ Ⓑ Ⓒ Ⓓ	97 Ⓐ Ⓑ Ⓒ Ⓓ
23 Ⓐ Ⓑ Ⓒ Ⓓ	48 Ⓐ Ⓑ Ⓒ Ⓓ	73 Ⓐ Ⓑ Ⓒ Ⓓ	98 Ⓐ Ⓑ Ⓒ Ⓓ
24 Ⓐ Ⓑ Ⓒ Ⓓ	49 Ⓐ Ⓑ Ⓒ Ⓓ	74 Ⓐ Ⓑ Ⓒ Ⓓ	99 Ⓐ Ⓑ Ⓒ Ⓓ
25 Ⓐ Ⓑ Ⓒ Ⓓ	50 Ⓐ Ⓑ Ⓒ Ⓓ	75 Ⓐ Ⓑ Ⓒ Ⓓ	100 Ⓐ Ⓑ Ⓒ Ⓓ

MILLER ANALOGIES SAMPLE TEST II

Directions: Each of these test questions consists of three CAPI-TALIZED words and four lettered words enclosed in parentheses. Two of the capitalized words are related in some way. Find the two related words and establish the nature of the relationship. Then study the four words lettered a, b, c and d. Select the one lettered word which is related to the remaining capitalized word in the same way that the first two capitalized words are related. Mark the Answer Sheet for the letter preceding the word you select.

1. CLOY : (a. collect, b. empty, c. glut, d. spoil) :: ARROGATE : USURP

2. ROBBERY : INCARCERATION :: (a. marking, b. singing, c. sleeping, d. embezzlement) : APPLAUSE

3. ICHTHYOLOGY : (a. insects, b. mammals, c. fish, d. invertebrates) :: ORNITHOLOGY : BIRDS

4. FIRST : PENULTIMATE :: JANUARY : (a. December, b. November, c. February, d. June)

5. HOPE : DESPONDENCY :: PLEASURE : (a. frolic, b. fun, c. joy, d. sadness)

6. DICHOTOMY : DIVISION :: DISSEMBLE : (a. feign, b. assemble, c. resemble, d. return)

7. LONGFELLOW : WHITMAN :: (a. Tagore, b. Keats, c. Heine, d. Dickens) : TENNYSON

8. MITER : BISHOP :: (a. stole, b. cleric, c. robe, d. biretta) : PRIEST

9. OK : KS :: PA : (a. CT, b. AZ, c. WV, d. NY)

10. SEED : BREED :: (a. origin, b. specimen, c. need, d. act) : DEED

11. (a. influence, b. compose, c. touch, d. infect) : RESULT :: AFFECT : EFFECT

12. SAUTEEING : COOKERY :: FAGOTING : (a. juggling, b. forestry, c. embroidery, d. medicine)

13. CAMPHOR : AROMATIC :: LILAC : (a. lavender, b. flower, c. fragrant, d. rose)

14. (a. skiers, b. winter, c. athletes, d. blades) : SKATES :: RUNNERS : SLEDS

15. LOCARNO : SWITZERLAND :: ARGONNE : (a. France, b. Quebec, c. Germany, d. Belgium)

16. ARMY : DEFENSE :: FOOD : (a. digestion, b. vegetation, c. nutrition, d. supply)

17. DAVID : (a. Matthew, b. Moses, c. Luke, d. Peter) :: RUTH : JEZEBEL

18. BENEFICENT : DELETERIOUS :: INIMICAL : (a. amicable, b. hostile, c. matchless, d. ordinary)

19. ANEMOMETER : (a. smell, b. airspeed, c. wind, d. pressure) :: ODOMETER : DISTANCE

20. WHIP : CRACK :: COURSE : (a. register, b. destroy, c. refine, d. precede)

21. HILL : MOUNTAIN :: (a. depression, b. discomfort, c. headache, d. fear) : PAIN

22. (a. The Merry Widow, b. Naughty Marietta, c. Iolanthe, d. Carmen) : MIKADO :: PINAFORE : GONDOLIERS

23. INCH : PINCH :: ANTS : (a. rants, b. dance, c. pants, d. pain)

24. WHEEL : COG :: (a. heaven, b. ribbon, c. rim, d. bulb) : FILAMENT

25. POLICEMAN : (a. convict, b. justice, c. conduct, d. crime) :: DENTIST : CAVITY

26. ROUND : CHUCK :: (a. circle, b. flank, c. chipped, d. throw) : RIB

27. FRACTIOUS : SYSTEMATIC :: DEBILITATE : (a. invigorate, b. undermine, c. diverge, d. annul)

28. FOUR : TWENTY :: (a. two, b. five, c. three, d. seven) : FIFTEEN

29. ENGINEER : SEMAPHORE :: PILOT : (a. radio, b. airplane, c. stewardess, d. copilot)

30. GLAND : ENDOCRINE :: MUSCLE : (a. hard, b. strong, c. dessicated, d. striated)

31. PROHIBITED : BANNED :: CANONICAL : (a. reputable, b. authoritative, c. referred, d. considered)

32. VIXEN : SEAMSTRESS :: BACCHUS : (a. Ceres, b. Neptune, c. Venus, d. Minerva)

33. ICE : STEAM :: BRICK : (a. straw, b. mortar, c. pole, d. gas)

34. BREATHING : (a. oxygen, b. lungs, c. carbon dioxide, d. nose) :: CRYING : TEARS

35. MARRIAGE : HASTE :: REPENT : (a. contrition, b. delay, c. leisure, d. deliberate)

36. JAMES I : (a. James II, b. George I, c. Elizabeth I, d. Charles I) :: GEORGE V : EDWARD VI

37. PLANS : ARCHITECT :: TREACHERY : (a. thief, b. traitor, c. cheater, d. killer)

38. LILY : PURITY :: (a. violet, b. lilac, c. poppy, d. ivy) : SLEEP

39. KEY : CHAIN :: ANCHOR : (a. dock, b. boat, c. prow, d. keel)

40. (a. miser, b. sandwich, c. surprise, d. tight) : SCROOGE :: LYNCH : GUILLOTINE

41. (a. subterranean, b. subconscious, c. superb, d. advertised) : SUB-LIMINAL :: PLETHORIC : SUPERFLUOUS

42. VICTORY : PYRRHIC :: FRUIT : (a. ripe, b. bitter, c. pie, d. tree)

43. TOUCH : DOWN :: (a. walk, b. river, c. home, d. stocking) : RUN

44. MITOSIS : DIVISION :: OSMOSIS : (a. diffusion, b. concentration, c. digestion, d. metamorphosis)

45. SUN : (a. summer, b. tan, c. parasol, d. beach) :: COLD : OVERCOAT

46. PHOEBUS : (a. Helius, b. Eos, c. Diana, d. Perseus) :: SUN : MOON

47. (a. equality, b. generous, c. wantonness, d. goodness) : LIBERTINE :: ADVOCACY : LAWYER

48. POUND : WEIGHT :: KILOGRAM : (a. weight, b. area, c. volume, d. capacity)

49. PRECARIOUS : CERTAIN :: ZEALOUS : (a. apathetic, b. ardent, c. indigent, d. sensitive)

50. PONDER : THOUGHT :: ARBITRATE : (a. endorsement, b. plan, c. argument, d. settlement)

51. OBSTRUCT : IMPEDE :: IMPENETRABLE : (a. forebearing, b. hidden, c. impervious, d. merciful)

52. OCTAVE : SESTET :: (a. scale, b. ending, c. quatrain, d. symphony) : COUPLET

53. NOVEL : (a. epic, b. drama, c. volume, d. story) :: TOM SAWYER : AENEID

54. PURSER : (a. bank, b. ship, c. race track, d. highway) :: BRAKEMAN : TRAIN

55. DRINK : THIRST :: SECURITY : (a. assuredness, b. stocks, c. fear, d. money)

56. CIRCLE : OVAL :: (a. figure, b. octagon, c. starfish, d. semicircle) : PARALLELOGRAM

57. RESILIENCY : RUBBER :: LAMBENCY : (a. oil, b. sheep, c. candlelight, d. lawn)

58. VIRTUOSO : (a. orchestra, b. home, c. prison, d. college) :: TEACHER : CLASSROOM

59. PLATEN : (a. newspaper, b. algae, c. ribbon, d. giant) :: COMB : COMPACT

60. (a. 4, b. 7, c. 9, d. 14) : 28 :: 11 : 44

61. CAPE : PROMONTORY :: WADI : (a. gully, b. waterfall, c. meadow, d. fen)

62. BINDING : BOOK :: WELDING : (a. box, b. tank, c. chair, d. wire)

63. SERFDOM : FEUDALISM :: ENTREPRENEURSHIP : (a. laissez faire, b. captain, c. radical, d. capitalism)

64. (a. bassos, b. dynamos, c. heroes, d. solos) : EMBARGOES :: VOLCANOES : TOMATOES

65. FOAL : HORSE :: CYGNET : (a. ring, b. fish, c. swan, d. constellation)

66. FRANCHISE : (a. license, b. commerce, c. separate, d. freedom) :: TYRANNY : DISSENT

67. HOUSE : BUILD :: TRENCH : (a. dig, b. trap, c. obliterate, d. dry)

68. CELL : WORKER :: ORGANISM : (a. occupation, b. proletariat, c. product, d. nation)

69. ANGLO-SAXON : ENGLISH :: LATIN : (a. Roman, b. Greek, c. Italian, d. Mediterranean)

70. METRO : (a. Paris, b. Rome, c. Moscow, d. Tokyo) :: UNDER-GROUND : LONDON

71. FETISH : TALISMAN :: FEALTY : (a. allegiance, b. faithlessness, c payment, d. real estate)

72. ACCELERATOR : (a. cylinder, b. inertia, c. motion, d. exhaust) :: CATALYST : CHANGE

73. INTELLIGENCE : UNDERSTANDING :: CONFUSION : (a. bemusement, b. pleasure, c. school, d. unhappiness)

74. TALKING : YELLING :: GIGGLING : (a. rejoicing, b. laughing, c. chuckling, d. sneering)

75. 49 : 7 :: (a. 98, b. 103, c. 94, d. 144) : 12

76. (a. Chrysler, b. mink, c. chauffeur, d. Boeing) : CADILLAC :: BEAVER : CHEVROLET

77. BREAK : BROKEN :: FLY : (a. flied, b. flew, c. flown, d. flying)

78. DEFALCATE : EMBEZZLEMENT :: EXCULPATE : (a. blame, b. uncover, c. exoneration, d. divulge)

79. SAW : (a. teeth, b. knife, c. board, d. blade) :: SCISSORS : CLOTH

80. PEDAL : PIANO :: BRIDGE : (a. case, b. tune, c. rosin, d. violin)

81. BUCOLIC : PEACEFUL :: CIMMERIAN : (a. warlike, b. tenebrous, c. doubtful, d. smirking)

82. FLATTERY : (a. praise, b. self-interest, c. honesty, d. openness) :: FLIGHT : SAFETY

83. PRAYER : (a. church, b. bible, c. religion, d. fulfillment) :: RESEARCH : DISCOVERY

84. PAYMENT : DEBT :: PREMIUM : (a. cracker, b. prize, c. insurance, d. scarcity)

85. SACRIFICE : HIT :: STEAL : (a. leave, b. slay, c. walk, d. rob)

86. (a. clap, b. play, c. doom, d. fork) : MOOD :: SLEEK : KEELS

87. DEMOLISH : BUILDING :: (a. sail, b. raze, c. dock, d. scuttle) : SHIP

88. LOGGIA : GALLERY :: JALOUSIE : (a. lintel, b. dowel, c. jamb, d. louver)

89. PAGE : CUB :: (a. book, b. paper, c. herald, d. knight) : REPORTER

90. VIRGO : TAURUS :: SEPTEMBER : (a. May, b. January, c. June, d. November)

91. FELICITY : BLISS :: CONGENIAL : (a. clever, b. compatible, c. fierce, d. unfriendly)

92. WHEEL : FENDER :: (a. paper, b. heading, c. letter, d. health) : SALUTATION

93. REQUEST : DEMAND :: VISIT : (a. return, b. welcome, c. invasion, d. house)

94. DENOUEMENT : (a. climax, b. outcome, c. complication, d. untying) :: DEBIT : CREDIT

95. STRAIGHT : POKER :: SMASH : (a. hit, b. tennis, c. ruin, d. bat)

96. MATES : TEAMS :: (a. heat, b. engine, c. vapor, d. meats) : STEAM

97. VALLEY : GORGE :: MOUNTAIN : (a. hill, b. cliff, c. acme, d. high)

98. ALPHA : OMEGA :: MERCURY : (a. Saturn, b. planet, c. Pluto, d. Venus)

99. CHIFFON : TWEED :: (a. synthetic, b. sheer, c. dark, d. textured) : ROUGH

100. SIDEREAL : (a. side, b. part, c. stars, d. planets) :: LUNAR : MOON

ANSWER KEY FOR MILLER ANALOGIES SAMPLE TEST II

1.	c	21.	b	41.	b	61.	a	81.	b
2.	b	22.	c	42.	b	62.	b	82.	b
3.	c	23.	c	43.	c	63.	d	83.	d
4.	b	24.	d	44.	a	64.	c	84.	c
5.	d	25.	d	45.	c	65.	c	85.	c
6.	a	26.	b	46.	c	66.	d	86.	c
7.	b	27.	a	47.	c	67.	a	87.	d
8.	d	28.	c	48.	a	68.	b	88.	d
9.	d	29.	a	49.	a	69.	c	89.	d
10.	c	30.	d	50.	d	70.	a	90.	a
11.	a	31.	b	51.	c	71.	a	91.	b
12.	c	32.	b	52.	c	72.	c	92.	b
13.	c	33.	d	53.	a	73.	a	93.	c
14.	d	34.	c	54.	b	74.	b	94.	c
15.	a	35.	c	55.	c	75.	d	95.	b
16.	c	36.	d	56.	b	76.	b	96.	d
17.	b	37.	b	57.	c	77.	c	97.	b
18.	a	38.	c	58.	a	78.	c	98.	c
19.	c	39.	b	59.	c	79.	c	99.	b
20.	a	40.	b	60.	b	80.	d	100.	c

EXPLANATORY ANSWERS FOR
MILLER ANALOGIES SAMPLE TEST II

1. **(c)** ARROGATE and USURP, which both mean to sieze without justification, are related as synonyms; the only synonym for CLOY meaning to satiate, is GLUT.

2. **(b)** This is a cause-and-effect analogy. ROBBERY can result in INCARCERATION, and SINGING can result in APPLAUSE.

3. **(c)** The relationship is one of classification. ICHTHYOLOGY is the study of FISH, and ORNITHOLOGY is the study of BIRDS.

4. **(b)** This is a sequence relationship. JANUARY is the FIRST month of a year, and NOVEMBER is the PENULTIMATE, or next to last, month of a year.

5. **(d)** HOPE and DESPONDENCY are contrasting concepts. The concept that contrasts with PLEASURE is SADNESS.

6. **(a)** DICHOTOMY and DIVISION are synonyms; a synonym for DISSEMBLE (meaning to disguise) is FEIGN.

7. (b) The relationship between LONGFELLOW and WHITMAN is that both of them were American poets. Since TENNYSON was an English poet the task is to determine who is another English poet. KEATS is the only choice; Dickens was an English writer, but a novelist.

8. (d) The analogy is one of association. A MITER is a head ornament usually worn by a BISHOP; a BIRETTA is a cap characteristically worn by a PRIEST. A stole and a robe might also be worn by a priest, but biretta more specifically completes the correspondence with miter.

9. (d) OK and KS are both proper post office abbreviations for states (Oklahoma and Kansas). Oklahoma is also on the southern border of Kansas; PA (Pennsylvania in post office abbreviation) is on the southern border of NY (New York).

10. (c) This is a non-semantic analogy. SEED, BREED, DEED and NEED all rhyme.

11. (a) This is an analogy of synonyms. AFFECT is a verb meaning to INFLUENCE. EFFECT as a noun means RESULT. (The verb effect means to bring about.)

12. (c) The relationship is one of action to object since SAUTEEING is one act or form of COOKERY; therefore, the task is to determine what FAGOTING is an act or form of. The correct answer is EMBROIDERY.

13. (c) AROMATIC is a characteristic of CAMPHOR; a characteristic of LILAC is FRAGRANT.

14. (d) This is a part-to-whole analogy. BLADES are parts of SKATES; RUNNERS are parts of SLEDS.

15. (a) The relationship is one of place. Since LOCARNO is located in SWITZERLAND, the task is to determine where ARGONNE is located, which is in France.

16. (c) This is a purpose analogy. A purpose of an ARMY is to provide DEFENSE; a purpose of FOOD is to provide NUTRITION.

17. (b) RUTH and JEZEBEL were both women who figured in the Old Testament. Since DAVID was a man in the Old Testament, the task is to find another man who was mentioned in the Old Testament. Moses is the correct choice.

18. (a) BENEFICIENT (beneficial) and DELETERIOUS (harmful) are antonyms. The only available antonym for INIMICAL (hostile) is AMICABLE (friendly).

19. (c) The analogy is one of measurement. An ODOMETER measures DISTANCE; an ANEMOMETER measures the velocity of the WIND.

20. (a) The relationship is one of object to action. One may CRACK a WHIP; one may REGISTER for a COURSE.

21. (b) In this analogy of degree, a HILL is a smaller version of a MOUNTAIN; DISCOMFORT is a lesser version of PAIN. Note that a headache and depression are specific types of pain or discomfort, not degrees.

22. (c) The relationship is one of classification. The MIKADO, PINAFORE and GONDOLIERS are all operettas written by Gilbert and Sullivan. IOLANTHE is the only other play among the four choices by this pair.

23. (c) In this non-semantic analogy, the letter P has been added to the word INCH, which forms the word PINCH: adding a P to ANTS forms PANTS.

24. (d) This is a part-to-whole relationship. A COG is part of a WHEEL just as a FILAMENT is part of a light BULB.

25. (d) One characteristic of a DENTIST is that he fights a CAVITY. Similarly, a characteristic of a POLICEMAN is that he fights CRIME.

26. (b) Every term in this analogy, ROUND, CHUCK and RIB, is a cut of beefsteak. Therefore, the missing term must be FLANK.

27. (a) The given pair are related as antonyms since FRACTIOUS means wild or unruly, the opposite of SYSTEMATIC. DEBILITATE, which means to weaken, must be paired with its opposite, INVIGORATE, which means to strengthen.

28. (c) In this numerical analogy, the relationship between FOUR and TWENTY is a one-to-five ratio; the number with the same ratio to FIFTEEN is THREE.

29. (a) The relationship is one of worker to tool. An ENGINEER may use a SEMAPHORE for communication; a PILOT may use a RADIO.

30. (d) ENDOCRINE is one type of GLAND; one type of MUSCLE is STRIATED.

31. (b) PROHIBITED and BANNED are related as synonyms; a synonym for CANONICAL is AUTHORITATIVE.

32. (b) The relationship between VIXEN and SEAMSTRESS is one of gender since both are female. Since BACCHUS is masculine (the Greek god of

wine), the task is to find another male among the answer choices, and NEPTUNE (the Roman god of the sea) is the only possibility.

33. (d) ICE is matter in the solid state, as opposed to STEAM, which is matter in the gaseous state. Similarly, BRICK is matter in the solid state and GAS is matter in the gaseous state.

34. (c) The relationship is action to object since CRYING releases TEARS. The task, then, is to determine what BREATHING releases. The process of respiration involves the intake of oxygen and the release of CARBON DIOXIDE.

35. (c) In this adage analogy, the familiar saying is MARRIAGE in HASTE. REPENT at LEISURE.

36. (d) The relationship is one of sequence. The English king EDWARD VI followed GEORGE V. To complete the analogy, the successor to JAMES I, CHARLES I, is the correct term.

37. (b) This is a worker-to-tool analogy since PLANS are the tool of the ARCHITECT as TREACHERY is the tool of the TRAITOR.

38. (c) In this symbol analogy, a LILY is a traditional symbol of PURITY just as a POPPY is a symbol of SLEEP.

39. (b) A KEY hangs from a CHAIN; an ANCHOR hangs from a BOAT.

40. (b) Every term in this analogy is a word derived from a person's name. SCROOGE comes from Dickens' Ebenezer Scrooge in *A Christmas Carol*; LYNCH, to put to death by mob action, comes from a Judge Lynch; a GUILLOTINE takes its name from Dr. Joseph Guillotin. Among the choices only SANDWICH describes both a thing and a person from which it takes its name. The Earl of Sandwich is said to have been the first to put meat between slices of bread.

41. (b) PLETHORIC and SUPERFLUOUS are synonyms for excess; a synonym for SUBLIMINAL is SUBCONSCIOUS, meaning outside the area of conscious awareness.

42. (b) A Pyrrhic victory is a bitter one since it means a victory gained at ruinous loss; therefore, PYRRHIC is an undesirable characteristic of VICTORY. A similar characteristic of FRUIT is BITTER.

43. (c) The relationship between TOUCH and DOWN is grammatical since these words can be used by themselves and also as a common sports-oriented compound word; therefore, the task is to determine which word can be used by itself and also as a common sports-oriented compound word with RUN. HOME is the correct choice.

44. (a) The relationship is one of part to whole. MITOSIS is one kind of DIVISION, specifically the series of processes that takes place in the nucleus of a dividing cell which results in the formation of two new nuclei each having the same number of chromosomes as the parent nucleus. OSMOSIS is one kind of DIFFUSION, specifically diffusion through a semipermeable membrane separating a solution of lesser solute concentration from one of greater concentration which tends to equalize the concentration of the two solutions.

45. (c) The purpose of an OVERCOAT is to protect one from the COLD; a PARASOL protects one from the SUN.

46. (c) This is a mythological analogy. PHEOBUS is the god of the SUN; DIANA is the goddess of the MOON.

47. (c) The relationship is one of characteristic. One characteristic of a LAWYER is his ADVOCACY or support of his client; a characteristic of a LIBERTINE, or one who leads a dissolute life, is WANTONNESS.

48. (a) This is a measurement analogy. A POUND is a measurement of WEIGHT; a KILOGRAM is also a measure of WEIGHT.

49. (a) PRECARIOUS and CERTAIN are antonyms; an antonym for ZEALOUS is APATHETIC.

50. (d) The correspondence is one of action to object. To PONDER aids THOUGHT: to ARBITRATE aids a SETTLEMENT.

51. (c) OBSTRUCT and IMPEDE are synonyms; a synonym for IMPENETRABLE is IMPERVIOUS.

52. (c) This is an anology of parts. OCTAVE, SESTET and COUPLET are all parts of a sonnet. Only QUATRAIN among the choices is also a part of a sonnet.

53. (a) The relationship between TOM SAWYER and the AENEID is one of classification. TOM SAWYER is a NOVEL and the AENEID is an EPIC.

54. (b) The correspondence is one of association. A BRAKEMAN is associated with a TRAIN; a PURSER is associated with a SHIP.

55. (c) A purpose of DRINK is to relieve THIRST; a purpose of SECURITY is to relieve FEAR.

56. (b) CIRCLE and OVAL are both figures enclosed with one continuous curved side; since a PARALLELOGRAM is a figure enclosed with straight sides, the task is to find another straight-sided figure. OCTAGON is the only available choice.

57. (c) RESILIENCY is a characteristic of RUBBER; LAMBENCY, which means brightness or flickering, is a characteristic of CANDLELIGHT.

58. (a) A TEACHER works in a CLASSROOM; therefore, the task is to determine where a VIRTUOSO works. Among the choices, an ORCHESTRA is the most likely place.

59. (c) In this part-to-part analogy, a COMB and a COMPACT are usually parts of the contents of a purse; a PLATEN, or roller, and a RIBBON are parts of a typewriter.

60. (b) The numerical relationship between 11 and 44 is a ratio of 1 to 4; therefore, the task is to determine what number when paired with 28 is also in the ratio of 1 to 4. The answer is 7.

61. (a) CAPE and PROMONTORY are synonyms meaning a point of land jutting into the sea; a synonym for WADI is GULLY.

62. (b) BINDING secures or holds together a BOOK; WELDING secures or holds together a TANK.

63. (d) SERFDOM is a characteristic of FEUDALISM; ENTREPRENEURSHIP is a characteristic of CAPITALISM.

64. (c) The relationship between VOLCANOES and TOMATOES is grammatical. Each is a plural formed by adding *es*. Since EMBARGOES is also a plural formed by adding *es*, the task is to find another word that also forms its plural this way. HEROES is the correct choice.

65. (c) A FOAL is a young HORSE; a CYGNET is a young SWAN. The relationship is one of young to old.

66. (d) This analogy is one of cause and effect. One effect of TYRANNY is DISSENT; an effect of a FRANCHISE, a right or immunity from some restriction, is FREEDOM.

67. (a) The relationship is object to action. A HOUSE is something to BUILD; a TRENCH is something to DIG.

68. (b) The correspondence is one of part to whole. A CELL is part of an ORGANISM; a WORKER is part of the PROLETARIAT. A worker may also be part of a nation. but PROLETARIAT is more specifically related to a WORKER.

69. (c) This is a sequence relationship. ANGLO-SAXON is an early form of ENGLISH; LATIN is an early form of ITALIAN.

70. (a) The subway in LONDON is called the UNDERGROUND; the subway in PARIS is called the METRO.

71. (a) FETISH and TALISMAN are synonyms; a synonym for FEALTY is ALLEGIANCE.

72. (c) The relationship is that of cause and effect as a CATALYST causes CHANGE and an ACCELERATOR causes MOTION.

73. (a) UNDERSTANDING is a characteristic of INTELLIGENCE; a characteristic of confusion is BEMUSEMENT. Unhappiness could also be a characteristic, but BEMUSEMENT is more specifically connected to CONFUSION.

74. (b) YELLING is a greater degree of TALKING; a greater degree of GIGGLING is LAUGHING.

75. (d) The numerical relationship between 49 and 7 is that 49 is the product of 7 multiplied by itself; therefore, the task is to determine the product of 12 multiplied by itself, or 144.

76. (b) The correspondence is one of similar types. CHEVROLET and CADILLAC are both types of automobiles; since a BEAVER is a type of animal, to complete the analogy another type of animal must be selected. MINK is the only available choice.

77. (c) In this grammatical analogy, the past participle of BREAK is BROKEN the past participle of FLY is FLOWN.

78. (c) This is an action-to-object analogy. To DEFALCATE is an act of EMBEZZLEMENT; to EXCULPATE is an act of EXONERATION.

79. (c) The relationship is one of purpose since the purpose of SCISSORS is to cut CLOTH just as the purpose of a SAW is to cut a BOARD.

80. (d) A PEDAL is part of a PIANO; a BRIDGE is part of a VIOLIN.

81. (b) BUCOLIC and PEACEFUL are synonyms since BUCOLIC refers to pastoral and peaceful scenes; a synonym of CIMMERIAN, meaning shrouded in gloom and darkness, is TENEBROUS.

82. (b) A purpose of FLIGHT is SAFETY; a purpose of FLATTERY is SELF-INTEREST.

83. (d) The relationship is one of purpose since the aim of RESEARCH is DISCOVERY; the aim of PRAYER is FULFILLMENT.

84. (c) The correspondence is one of association since PAYMENT is the term applied to money expended to reduce a DEBT just as PREMIUM is the term applied to money expended to obtain INSURANCE.

85. (c) SACRIFICE, HIT, and STEAL are all plays in baseball games. Among the choices only WALK is another type of baseball play.

86. (c) The relationship is non-semantic. SLEEK spelled backwards is KEELS; MOOD spelled backwards is DOOM.

87. (d) The relationship is action to object. To destroy a BUILDING you can DEMOLISH it; to destroy a SHIP you can SCUTTLE it.

88. (d) LOGGIA and GALLERY are both types of porches; since JALOUSIE is a type of blind, the task is to find another type of blind, and LOUVER is the correct choice.

89. (d) The relationship is one of degree. A CUB is a young REPORTER; a PAGE is a young KNIGHT.

90. (a) The zodiac sign VIRGO is associated with the month of SEPTEMBER; TAURUS is associated with MAY.

91. (b) FELICITY and BLISS are synonyms; a synonym for CONGENIAL is COMPATIBLE.

92. (b) Both WHEEL and FENDER are parts of a larger automotive unit; a SALUTATION and a HEADING are parts of a letter.

93. (c) The relationship is one of degree since a REQUEST is a polite term, and a DEMAND can be an unpleasant request. Since VISIT is a polite term, the task is to find a word that denotes an unpleasant visit. INVASION is the correct choice.

94. (c) DEBIT and CREDIT are antonyms; an antonym for DENOUEMENT is COMPLICATION.

95. (b) A STRAIGHT is a characteristic of a POKER game; a SMASH is a characteristic stroke in a game of TENNIS.

96. (d) MATES, TEAMS, and STEAM are all anagrams. MEATS is another anagram, which completes the analogy.

97. (b) A GORGE is a steep part of a VALLEY; a CLIFF is a steep part of a MOUNTAIN.

98. (c) The relationship is one of sequence. Just as ALPHA and OMEGA are the first and last letters in the Greek alphabet, MERCURY and PLUTO are the planets closest to and farthest from the sun.

99. (b) This analogy is one of characteristic. A characteristic of TWEED is that it is ROUGH; a characteristic of CHIFFON is that it is SHEER.

100. (c) The relationship is one of association. LUNAR is associated with the MOON; SIDEREAL is related to the STARS.

ANSWER SHEET FOR
MILLER ANALOGIES SAMPLE TEST III

1 Ⓐ Ⓑ Ⓒ Ⓓ	26 Ⓐ Ⓑ Ⓒ Ⓓ	51 Ⓐ Ⓑ Ⓒ Ⓓ	76 Ⓐ Ⓑ Ⓒ Ⓓ
2 Ⓐ Ⓑ Ⓒ Ⓓ	27 Ⓐ Ⓑ Ⓒ Ⓓ	52 Ⓐ Ⓑ Ⓒ Ⓓ	77 Ⓐ Ⓑ Ⓒ Ⓓ
3 Ⓐ Ⓑ Ⓒ Ⓓ	28 Ⓐ Ⓑ Ⓒ Ⓓ	53 Ⓐ Ⓑ Ⓒ Ⓓ	78 Ⓐ Ⓑ Ⓒ Ⓓ
4 Ⓐ Ⓑ Ⓒ Ⓓ	29 Ⓐ Ⓑ Ⓒ Ⓓ	54 Ⓐ Ⓑ Ⓒ Ⓓ	79 Ⓐ Ⓑ Ⓒ Ⓓ
5 Ⓐ Ⓑ Ⓒ Ⓓ	30 Ⓐ Ⓑ Ⓒ Ⓓ	55 Ⓐ Ⓑ Ⓒ Ⓓ	80 Ⓐ Ⓑ Ⓒ Ⓓ
6 Ⓐ Ⓑ Ⓒ Ⓓ	31 Ⓐ Ⓑ Ⓒ Ⓓ	56 Ⓐ Ⓑ Ⓒ Ⓓ	81 Ⓐ Ⓑ Ⓒ Ⓓ
7 Ⓐ Ⓑ Ⓒ Ⓓ	32 Ⓐ Ⓑ Ⓒ Ⓓ	57 Ⓐ Ⓑ Ⓒ Ⓓ	82 Ⓐ Ⓑ Ⓒ Ⓓ
8 Ⓐ Ⓑ Ⓒ Ⓓ	33 Ⓐ Ⓑ Ⓒ Ⓓ	58 Ⓐ Ⓑ Ⓒ Ⓓ	83 Ⓐ Ⓑ Ⓒ Ⓓ
9 Ⓐ Ⓑ Ⓒ Ⓓ	34 Ⓐ Ⓑ Ⓒ Ⓓ	59 Ⓐ Ⓑ Ⓒ Ⓓ	84 Ⓐ Ⓑ Ⓒ Ⓓ
10 Ⓐ Ⓑ Ⓒ Ⓓ	35 Ⓐ Ⓑ Ⓒ Ⓓ	60 Ⓐ Ⓑ Ⓒ Ⓓ	85 Ⓐ Ⓑ Ⓒ Ⓓ
11 Ⓐ Ⓑ Ⓒ Ⓓ	36 Ⓐ Ⓑ Ⓒ Ⓓ	61 Ⓐ Ⓑ Ⓒ Ⓓ	86 Ⓐ Ⓑ Ⓒ Ⓓ
12 Ⓐ Ⓑ Ⓒ Ⓓ	37 Ⓐ Ⓑ Ⓒ Ⓓ	62 Ⓐ Ⓑ Ⓒ Ⓓ	87 Ⓐ Ⓑ Ⓒ Ⓓ
13 Ⓐ Ⓑ Ⓒ Ⓓ	38 Ⓐ Ⓑ Ⓒ Ⓓ	63 Ⓐ Ⓑ Ⓒ Ⓓ	88 Ⓐ Ⓑ Ⓒ Ⓓ
14 Ⓐ Ⓑ Ⓒ Ⓓ	39 Ⓐ Ⓑ Ⓒ Ⓓ	64 Ⓐ Ⓑ Ⓒ Ⓓ	89 Ⓐ Ⓑ Ⓒ Ⓓ
15 Ⓐ Ⓑ Ⓒ Ⓓ	40 Ⓐ Ⓑ Ⓒ Ⓓ	65 Ⓐ Ⓑ Ⓒ Ⓓ	90 Ⓐ Ⓑ Ⓒ Ⓓ
16 Ⓐ Ⓑ Ⓒ Ⓓ	41 Ⓐ Ⓑ Ⓒ Ⓓ	66 Ⓐ Ⓑ Ⓒ Ⓓ	91 Ⓐ Ⓑ Ⓒ Ⓓ
17 Ⓐ Ⓑ Ⓒ Ⓓ	42 Ⓐ Ⓑ Ⓒ Ⓓ	67 Ⓐ Ⓑ Ⓒ Ⓓ	92 Ⓐ Ⓑ Ⓒ Ⓓ
18 Ⓐ Ⓑ Ⓒ Ⓓ	43 Ⓐ Ⓑ Ⓒ Ⓓ	68 Ⓐ Ⓑ Ⓒ Ⓓ	93 Ⓐ Ⓑ Ⓒ Ⓓ
19 Ⓐ Ⓑ Ⓒ Ⓓ	44 Ⓐ Ⓑ Ⓒ Ⓓ	69 Ⓐ Ⓑ Ⓒ Ⓓ	94 Ⓐ Ⓑ Ⓒ Ⓓ
20 Ⓐ Ⓑ Ⓒ Ⓓ	45 Ⓐ Ⓑ Ⓒ Ⓓ	70 Ⓐ Ⓑ Ⓒ Ⓓ	95 Ⓐ Ⓑ Ⓒ Ⓓ
21 Ⓐ Ⓑ Ⓒ Ⓓ	46 Ⓐ Ⓑ Ⓒ Ⓓ	71 Ⓐ Ⓑ Ⓒ Ⓓ	96 Ⓐ Ⓑ Ⓒ Ⓓ
22 Ⓐ Ⓑ Ⓒ Ⓓ	47 Ⓐ Ⓑ Ⓒ Ⓓ	72 Ⓐ Ⓑ Ⓒ Ⓓ	97 Ⓐ Ⓑ Ⓒ Ⓓ
23 Ⓐ Ⓑ Ⓒ Ⓓ	48 Ⓐ Ⓑ Ⓒ Ⓓ	73 Ⓐ Ⓑ Ⓒ Ⓓ	98 Ⓐ Ⓑ Ⓒ Ⓓ
24 Ⓐ Ⓑ Ⓒ Ⓓ	49 Ⓐ Ⓑ Ⓒ Ⓓ	74 Ⓐ Ⓑ Ⓒ Ⓓ	99 Ⓐ Ⓑ Ⓒ Ⓓ
25 Ⓐ Ⓑ Ⓒ Ⓓ	50 Ⓐ Ⓑ Ⓒ Ⓓ	75 Ⓐ Ⓑ Ⓒ Ⓓ	100 Ⓐ Ⓑ Ⓒ Ⓓ

MILLER ANALOGIES SAMPLE TEST III

Directions: Each of these test questions consists of three CAPI-TALIZED words and four lettered words enclosed in parentheses. Two of the capitalized words are related in some way. Find the two related words and establish the nature of the relationship. Then study the four words lettered a, b, c and d. Select the one lettered word which is related to the remaining capitalized word in the same way that the first two capitalized words are related. Mark the Answer Sheet for the letter preceding the word you select.

1. SCEPTER : AUTHORITY :: SCALES (a. weight, b. justice, c. commerce, d. greed)

2. DEJECTION : (a. carelessness, b. failure, c. prostration, d. ineptitude) :: VANITY : COMPLACENCY

3. WORM : BIRD :: MOUSE : (a. man, b. snake, c. rodent, d. cheese)

4. (a. artist, b. description, c. narration, d. personality) : CHARACTERIZATION :: PICTURE : PORTRAIT

5. (a. orate, b. sing, c. mumble, d. speak) : TALK :: SCRAWL : WRITE

6. LYNDON JOHNSON : JOHN F. KENNEDY :: ANDREW JOHNSON : (a. Ulysses S. Grant, b. Abraham Lincoln, c. Martin Van Buren, d. William Pierce)

7. 15 : 6 :: 23 : (a. 8, b. 7, c. 6, d. 5)

8. STEAM : WATER :: (a. lake, b. cloud, c. salt, d. tide) : OCEAN

9. SODIUM : SALT :: OXYGEN : (a. acetylene, b. carbon tetrachloride, c. water, d. ammonia)

10. (a. theft, b. notoriety, c. police, d. jail) : CRIME :: CEMETERY : DEATH

11. GRASS : (a. cow, b. onion, c. lettuce, d. earth) :: SNOW : MILK

12. HAND : (a. girth, b. fingers, c. horse, d. glove) :: LIGHT-YEAR : SPACE

13. ARGUMENT : DEBATE :: FIGHT : (a. skirmish, b. contest, c. challenge, d. crisis)

14. PICCOLO : (a. trumpet, b. trombone, c. horn, d. alto saxophone) :: VIOLIN : BASS

77

15. DIVULGE : DISCLOSE :: APPRAISAL : (a. revision, b. respite, c. continuation, d. estimate)

16. WEALTH : TANGIBLE :: (a. price, b. gold, c. success, d. gifts) :INTANGIBLE

17. HEMOGLOBIN : BLOOD :: COACHES : (a. train, b. whip, c. fuel, d. road)

18. SHELTER : (a. refuge, b. cave, c. mansion, d. protection) :: BREAD : CAKE

19. AFFLUENT : (a. charity, b. luck, c. misfortune, d. indifference) :: IMPOVERISHED : LAZINESS

20. INNING : BASEBALL :: (a. time, b. date, c. era, d. chronology) : HISTORY

21. SHONE : DISHONEST :: LEST : (a. many, b. tool, c. candlestick, d. lamp)

22. (a. stifle, b. tell, c. joke, d. offer) : LAUGH :: THROW : JAVELIN

23. CHARLESTON : (a. Tucson, b. Springfield, c. Williamsburg, d. Chicago) :: BOSTON : PHILADELPHIA

24. VINTNER : MINER :: (a. vines, b. wine, c. liquid, d. grape) : ORE

25. (a. jaguar, b. mink, c. cougar, d. chinchilla) : GIRAFFE :: TIGER : ZEBRA

26. (a. Athene, b. Artemis, c. Hera, d. Medea) : FRIGGA :: ZEUS : ODIN

27. DREDGE : SCOOP :: (a. barge, b. slow, c. field, d. channel) : ICE CREAM

28. LIMP : CANE :: (a. cell, b. muscle, c. heat, d. cold) : TISSUE

29. CONFESSOR : KINGMAKER :: EDWARD : (a. Warwick, b. Alfred, c. George, d. Gloucester)

30. (a. parchment, b. concrete, c. cardboard, d. timber) : ADOBE :: PAPER : PAPYRUS

31. HANDS : ARMS :: (a. Vulcan, b. idleness, c. Diana, d. destiny) : MORPHEUS

32. HYMN : THEIR :: CELL : (a. score, b. peal, c. tree, d. mile)

33. DOG : SWAN :: (a. bark, b. noise, c. days, d. collie) : SONG

34. EINSTEIN : MALTHUS :: RELATIVITY : (a. population, b. religion, c. economy, d. democracy)

35. GALLEY : ROOKERY :: MEAL : (a. bird, b. seal, c. peal, d. chess)

36. PEACH : (a. apple, b. beet, c. grape, d. tomato) :: CHERRY : RADISH

37. LASSITUDE : (a. longitude, b. languor, c. purity, d. alacrity) :: PARSIMONY : BENEFACTION

38. THERMOSTAT : REGULATE :: (a. draft, b. windows, c. insulation, d. thermometer) : CONSERVE

39. CLOTH : FLAG :: (a. dress, b. object, c. covering, d. badge) : SYMBOL

40. (a. earth, b. Venus, c. Sputnik, d. berry) : PLANET :: CANAL : RIVER

41. PIREAUS : OSTIA :: (a. Athens, b. Florence, c. Milan, d. Crete) : ROME

42. (a. psychology, b. philology, c. philosophy, d. philately) : PHRE-NOLOGY :: ASTRONOMY : ASTROLOGY

43. ORACLE : LOGICIAN :: INTUITION : (a. guess, b. syllogism, c. faith, d. theory)

44. STUDENT : DEW :: SIEVE : (a. reprieve, b. relieve, c. receive, d. give)

45. GERONTOLOGY : GENEALOGY :: (a. families, b. aging, c. gerunds, d. birth) : LINEAGE

46. ROMAN : (a. Caesar, b. Rembrandt, c. gladiator, d. Van Dyke) :: NOSE : BEARD

47. HYDROGEN : 1 :: (a. carbon, b. oxygen, c. nitrogen, d. potassium) : 16

48. (a. promontory, b. bridge, c. nib, d. empty) : RESERVOIR :: ARCH : HEEL

49. 19 : 23 :: (a. 7, b. 11, c. 13, d. 17) : 13

50. PANORAMA : CHURCH DOOR : ABYSS : (a. truth, b. bond, c. speck, d. ocean)

51. (a. Laos, b. Indonesia, c. Afghanistan, d. Japan) : INDIA :: NEVADA : COLORADO

52. CONCISE : (a. refined, b. expanded, c. precise, d. blunt) : REMOVE : OBLITERATE

53. TRAINING : ACUMEN :: (a. stupidity, b. experience, c. hunger, d. restlessness) : INANITION

54. BANTAM : (a. fly, b. chicken, c. fowl, d. small) :: WELTER : LIGHT

55. JACKET : (a. lapel, b. button, c. vest, d. dinner) :: PANTS : CUFF

56. (a. grave, b. aggravated, c. theft, d. first degree) : GRAND :: ASSAULT : LARCENY

57. (a. Athena, b. Ceres, c. Artemis, d. Aphrodite) : ZEUS :: EVE : ADAM

58. SERAPHIC : (a. Napoleonic, b. Mephistophelian, c. Alexandrine, d. euphoric) :: IMPROVIDENT : PRESCIENT

59. STRIPES : (a. bars, b. oak leaf, c. stars, d. general) :: SERGEANT : MAJOR

60. (a. precarious, b. deleterious, c. deterred, d. immortal) : DEADLY :: CELEBRATED : LIONIZED

61. MANET : REMBRANDT :: (a. Picasso, b. Dali, c. Pollock, d. Cezanne) : VAN GOGH

62. (a. glove, b. stocking, c. weakness, d. mitt) : GAUNTLET :: HAT : HELMET

63. STAPES : COCHLEA :: BRIM : (a. hat, b. derby, c. crown, d. head)

64. (a. rococo, b. severe, c. Etruscan, d. stylish) : ORNAMENTED :: SOGGY : MOIST

65. BURSAR : (a. funds, b. semester, c. accounts, d. purse) :: SEMINAR : IVY

66. NEW YORK : RHODES :: LIBERTY : (a. Apollo, b. scholar, c. tyranny, d. freedom)

67. RUBY : EMERALD :: TOMATO : (a. rose, b. onion, c. peach, d. lettuce)

68. SOLID : MELTING :: SOLUTION : (a. saturation, b. liquefaction, c heating, d. mixing)

69. (a. royal, b. kingly, c. regal, d. princely) : LAGER :: TIME : EMIT

70. HENRY FIELDING : (a. Victorian, b. Romantic, c. Restoration, d. Augustan) :: BEN JONSON : ELIZABETHAN

71. ARKANSAS : FLORIDA :: NEW MEXICO : (a. Tennessee, b. Ohio, c. California, d. Illinois)

72. SIN : ATONEMENT :: (a. clemency, b. peace, c. war, d. virtue) : REPARATION

73. (a. solo, b. duet, c. trio, d. quartet) : QUINTET :: PRIZEFIGHT : BASKETBALL

74. PIPE : POT :: (a. scrub, b. ream, c. scourge, d. drain) : SCOUR

75. (a. echo, b. elephant, c. page, d. blue) : MEMORY :: DENIM : WALLPAPER

76. (a. Jupiter, b. Hippocrates, c. Cadmus, d. Ptolemy) : HANNIBAL :: CADUCEUS : SWORD

77. RADAR : DEPT. :: (a. telephone, b. radio, c. laser, d. telegraph) :: ACCT.

78. EPISTEMOLOGY : (a. letters, b. weapons, c. knowledge, d. roots) :: PALEONTOLOGY : FOSSILS

79. (a. ear, b. foundry, c. corps, d. fife) : DRUM :: FLINT : STEEL

80. CABER : (a. run, b. pass, c. mount, d. toss) :: EYE : BLINK

81. PLATO : (a. Socrates, b. Sophocles, c. Aristophanes, d. Aristotle) :: FREUD : JUNG

82. (a. law, b. book, c. band, d. wagon) : WAINWRIGHT :: DICTIONARY : LEXICOGRAPHER

83. RETIRE : REPRISE :: (a. sleep, b. face, c. program, d. return) : PROFILE

84. CONCERT : (a. andante, b. a cappella, c. opera, d. artistry) :: PER-FORMANCE : PANTOMIME

85. (a. uniform, b. commander, c. platoon, d. sentry) : DOG :: GARRISON : FLOCK

86. PORTUGAL : IBERIA :: TOOTH : (a. dentist, b. cavity, c. nail, d. comb)

87. RADIUS : (a. circle, b. arc, c. chord, d. diameter) :: YARD : FATHOM

88. EMINENT : LOWLY :: FREQUENT : (a. often, b. frivolous, c. rare, d. soon)

89. FILIGREE : METAL :: (a. lace, b. linen, c. cotton, d. silk) : THREAD

90. INTAGLIO : (a. cameo, b. caviar, c. Machiavellian, d. harem) :: CONCAVE : CONVEX

91. MEZZANINE : (a. orchestra, b. stage, c. proscenium, d. second balcony) :: ABDOMEN : THORAX

92. BULBOUS : GAUNT :: (a. unruly, b. onerous, c. tractable, d. strong) : CONTUMACIOUS

93. GLACIER : MOLASSES :: (a. dirge, b. moth, c. spring, d. mountain) : TORTOISE

94. FOLD : (a. fell, b. hand, c. falls, d. boat) :: FORD : STREAM

95. VERDI : (a. La Traviata, b. Fidelio, c. Aïda, d. Rigoletto) :: CHOPIN : PARSIFAL

96. SUBSTITUTE : TEAM :: UNDERSTUDY : (a. school, b. congregation, c. actor, d. cast)

97. PORT : (a. vintage, b. harbor, c. starboard, d. left) :: HEADLIGHTS : TRUNK

98. YORKTOWN : VICKSBURG :: CONCORD : (a. Philadelphia, b. Providence, c. Antietam, d. Valley Forge)

99. (a. fish, b. breath, c. pint, d. quart) : GILL :: OCTAVE : MONOTHEISM

100. ROOSTER : (a. crow, b. coop, c. egg, d. owl) :: EFFERVESCENT : EFFETE

ANSWER KEY FOR MILLER ANALOGIES SAMPLE TEST III

1.	b	21.	c	41.	a	61.	d	81.	d
2.	c	22.	a	42.	a	62.	a	82.	d
3.	b	23.	c	43.	b	63.	c	83.	c
4.	b	24.	b	44.	d	64.	a	84.	b
5.	c	25.	a	45.	b	65.	b	85.	d
6.	b	26.	c	46.	d	66.	a	86.	d
7.	d	27.	d	47.	b	67.	d	87.	d
8.	b	28.	d	48.	c	68.	a	88.	c
9.	c	29.	a	49.	b	69.	c	89.	a
10.	d	30.	b	50.	d	70.	d	90.	a
11.	c	31.	d	51.	c	71.	c	91.	d
12.	c	32.	b	52.	d	72.	c	92.	c
13.	b	33.	c	53.	c	73.	a	93.	a
14.	d	34.	a	54.	a	74.	b	94.	b
15.	d	35.	a	55.	a	75.	a	95.	b
16.	c	36.	b	56.	b	76.	b	96.	d
17.	a	37.	d	57.	a	77.	c	97.	c
18.	c	38.	c	58.	b	78.	c	98.	c
19.	b	39.	b	59.	b	79.	d	99.	d
20.	c	40.	c	60.	b	80.	d	100.	d

EXPLANATORY ANSWERS FOR
MILLER ANALOGIES SAMPLE TEST III

1. (b) A SCEPTER is a symbol of AUTHORITY; SCALES are a symbol of JUSTICE.

2. (c) The relationship is one of cause and effect. An effect of VANITY is COMPLACENCY, and an effect of DEJECTION is PROSTRATION.

3. (b) A BIRD will eat a WORM; a SNAKE will eat a MOUSE.

4. (b) A CHARACTERIZATION is a type of DESCRIPTION, usually of a person; a PORTRAIT is a type of PICTURE, usually of a person.

5. (c) To MUMBLE is to TALK carelessly, thus making it difficult to be understood; to SCRAWL is to WRITE carelessly, thus making it difficult to be understood.

6. (b) LYNDON JOHNSON was a vice-president who succeeded JOHN F. KENNEDY following Kennedy's assassination. ANDREW JOHNSON was the vice-president under ABRAHAM LINCOLN who also succeeded him after Lincoln's assassination.

7. (d) In this mathematical analogy, $1 + 5 = 6$; $2 + 3 = 5$.

8. (b) This is an analogy of the gaseous to the liquid state of a substance. STEAM is the vapor form into which WATER is converted by heat. A CLOUD is the vapor form into which OCEAN water is converted by condensation.

9. (c) SODIUM is one of the elements of SALT; OXYGEN is one of the elements of WATER.

10. (d) In this analogy of cause and effect, a CRIME usually results in time spent in JAIL; DEATH usually results in burial in a CEMETERY.

11. (c) SNOW and MILK are related because they are both white; GRASS and LETTUCE are both green.

12. (c) This analogy is one of measurement. A LIGHT-YEAR is a unit of measurement in SPACE. A HAND is a unit of measurement (equal to four inches) used to determine the height of a HORSE.

13. (b) An ARGUMENT can be a formal or an informal DEBATE; a FIGHT can be a formal or an informal CONTEST.

14. (d) A VIOLIN is a small high-pitched string instrument; a BASS is a large low-pitched string instrument. Because a PICCOLO is a small high-pitched wind instrument, to complete the analogy a large low-pitched wind instrument must be selected. An ALTO SAXOPHONE is the correct choice.

15. (d) DIVULGE and DISCLOSE are synonyms; a synonym for AP-PRAISAL is ESTIMATE.

16. (c) The correspondence is one of characteristic. WEALTH is usually measured in TANGIBLE units; SUCCESS is often measured in IN-TANGIBLE units.

17. (a) In this analogy of a part to a whole, HEMOGLOBIN is a part of BLOOD; COACHES constitute a part of a TRAIN.

18. (c) BREAD and CAKE are related because the former is a necessity while the latter is a luxury; similarly a SHELTER is a necessity, and a MANSION is a luxury.

19. (b) In this cause-and-effect analogy, LUCK is one possible factor contributing to making one AFFLUENT; LAZINESS is one possible cause making a person IMPOVERISHED.

20. (c) The relationship is one of measurement. A division of a BASEBALL

game is an INNING; a phase of HISTORY is called an ERA.

21. (c) In this non-semantic word-within-a-word analogy, SHONE is contained in the word DISHONEST; the word LEST is contained in the word CANDLESTICK.

22. (a) This is an action-to-object analogy. One may THROW a JAVELIN and one may STIFLE, or repress, a LAUGH.

23. (c) In this place analogy, CHARLESTON, BOSTON and PHILADELPHIA are related because they were important colonial cities. Among the available choices, only WILLIAMSBURG was another colonial city.

24. (b) The correspondence is one of a worker to his job. A VINTNER produces or sells WINE; a MINER extracts ORE from the earth.

25. (a) A JAGUAR and GIRAFFE are related because both have spots; a TIGER and a ZEBRA are both striped.

26. (c) ZEUS was king of the gods in Greek mythology; HERA was his wife. ODIN was the supreme god in Norse mythology; FRIGGA was his wife.

27. (d) In this action-to-object analogy, one may DREDGE, or deepen, a CHANNEL; one may SCOOP ICE CREAM.

28. (d) A person with a LIMP is likely to use a CANE; a person with a COLD is likely to use a TISSUE.

29. (a) The correspondence is one of association. EDWARD was known as the CONFESSOR; WARWICK was known as the KINGMAKER.

30. (b) This is an analogy of sequence. CONCRETE has replaced ADOBE as a building material; PAPER has replaced PAPYRUS as a writing material.

31. (d) There is a well-known expression, "in the arms of Morpheus and in the hands of destiny." In this adage analogy, ARMS are associated, therefore, with MORPHEUS and HANDS are associated with DESTINY.

32. (b) Each of the given terms in this analogy has a homophone, a word pronounced the same but spelled differently: HYMN (him); THEIR (there); and CELL (sell). Among the choices, only PEAL has a homophone (peel).

33. (c) The relationship is one of association. We speak of a SWAN SONG, that is, a farewell appearance or final act, and DOG DAYS, a period of hot, sultry weather or stagnation and inactivity.

34. (a) The correspondence is between a thinker and the theory he is associated with. EINSTEIN developed the theory of RELATIVITY; MALTHUS is famous for his theory of POPULATION. Although Malthus was an economist, it is not his field but his theory that successfully completes this analogy.

35. (a) In this analogy of place, a GALLEY is where a MEAL is produced, usually on board a ship; a ROOKERY is where a BIRD is produced.

36. (b) A CHERRY is a type of fruit; a RADISH is a type of vegetable. Because a PEACH is a fruit, to complete the relationship a vegetable must be selected, and BEET is the correct choice. Although sometimes called a vegetable, a tomato is actually a fruit.

37. (d) The opposite of PARSIMONY, or stinginess, is BENEFACTION, which means charitable donation; an antonym for LASSITUDE, meaning listlessness, is ALACRITY, which means promptness of response.

38. (c) The purpose of a THERMOSTAT is to REGULATE room temperature; the purpose of INSULATION is to CONSERVE energy.

39. (b) A CLOTH is a concrete object as opposed to a FLAG that is concrete but also abstract, standing for a country or patriotism. An OBJECT is concrete, and a SYMBOL is both a thing and that which stands for something else.

40. (c) The correspondence is between man-made and natural objects. SPUTNIK is a man-made object which orbits; a PLANET is a natural object which orbits. Similarly, a CANAL is a man-made waterway, and a RIVER is a natural waterway.

41. (a) In this place analogy, PIRAEUS is a port city near ATHENS; OSTIA was a port city near ROME.

42. (a) Since ASTRONOMY and ASTROLOGY both deal with the stars, with astronomy being the accepted science and astrology a disputed or questionable science, the task is to find an accepted science similar to the disputed science of PHRENOLOGY (which deals with the head). PSYCHOLOGY is the correct choice.

43. (b) The correspondence is one of thinker to tool. An ORACLE's prophecies are based on INTUITION; a LOGICIAN may reason by means of a SYLLOGISM, a formal scheme of deductive thinking.

44. (d) In this non-semantic analogy, STUDENT has the same initial vowel sound as DEW; SIEVE has the same vowel sound as GIVE.

45. (b) The relationship is one of classification. GERONTOLOGY is the study of AGING; GENEALOGY is the study of LINEAGE.

46. (d) We speak of a ROMAN NOSE and a VAN DYKE BEARD. The correspondence is one of association.

47. (b) HYDROGEN, the lightest element, has an atomic weight of 1. OXYGEN, with 8 protons and 8 neutrons in its nucleus, has an atomic weight of 16.

48. (c) The relationship is one of part to part. An ARCH and a HEEL are parts of a foot; a NIB and a RESERVOIR are parts of a pen.

49. (b) A prime number is one which has no factors which yield quotients other than 1 or itself. Although all the terms given are prime numbers, the correct choice also depends on a sequence. The next prime number after 19 is 23; similarly, the next prime number after 11 is 13.

50. (d) A characteristic of a PANORAMA and a CHURCH DOOR is that they are both wide; an ABYSS and an OCEAN are characteristically deep.

51. (c) In this analogy of place, NEVADA and COLORADO are states separated by another state, Utah. INDIA and AFGHANISTAN are countries separated by another country, Pakistan.

52. (d) REMOVE and OBLITERATE are synonyms having the same result of elimination, but varying in degree. One must, therefore, find another word for CONCISE that has the same result, yet varies in degree. Concise means succinct or pithy; BLUNT is a synonym but has a stronger connotation of brusqueness or rudeness.

53. (c) In this cause-and-effect analogy, TRAINING results in ACUMEN or keenness of perception or discernment. Similarly, HUNGER results in INANITION, a loss of vitality from absence of food and water.

54. (a) BANTAM, WELTER, LIGHT and FLY are all weight divisions in boxing.

55. (a) A LAPEL is a folded-over part of a JACKET; a CUFF is a folded-over part of a pair of PANTS.

56. (b) ASSAULT and LARCENY are both legal terms for crimes. GRAND corresponds to LARCENY, describing the degree of the crime. The term which indicates the degree of ASSAULT is AGGRAVATED.

57. (a) In this analogy of association, ATHENA is said to have sprung from the head of ZEUS; EVE is said to have been made from the rib of ADAM.

58. (b) IMPROVIDENT and PRESCIENT are related as antonyms. The former relates to the inability and the latter to the ability to foresee the

future. Similarly, the opposite of SERAPHIC, which means angelic, is MEPHISTOPHELIAN, which means devilish.

59. (b) In the army, STRIPES are associated with the rank of SERGEANT; an OAK LEAF is associated with the rank of MAJOR.

60. (b) In this cause-and-effect analogy, something that is DELETERIOUS (exceedingly harmful) may prove DEADLY; a person who is CELEBRATED (widely known) may be LIONIZED.

61. (d) MANET was a French painter and REMBRANDT was a Dutch painter. Because VAN GOGH is also a Dutch painter, to complete the analogy a French painter must be selected. The correct choice is CEZANNE.

62. (a) A HAT is a head covering worn in peace and a HELMET is a head covering worn in war; since GAUNTLET is a hand covering worn in war, one must look for a hand covering that is worn in peace, a GLOVE.

63. (c) The STAPES and the COCHLEA are parts of an ear; a BRIM and a CROWN are parts of a hat.

64. (a) The relationship is one of degree. ROCOCO means excessively ORNAMENTED; SOGGY means excessively MOIST.

65. (b) A BURSAR, SEMINAR and IVY are all things associated with college. To complete the analogy another term associated with college must be selected; that term is SEMESTER.

66. (a) The statue of LIBERTY is set at the entrance to the harbor of NEW YORK; a statue of APOLLO was set at the entrance to the harbor of ancient RHODES.

67. (d) A RUBY is a red gem and an EMERALD is green; a TOMATO is red and LETTUCE is green.

68. (a) In this measurement analogy, the MELTING point is an important measure of a SOLID; the SATURATION point is an important measurement of a SOLUTION.

69. (c) In this non-semantic analogy, REGAL spelled backwards is LAGER; TIME spelled backwards is EMIT.

70. (d) The correspondence is one of association. BEN JONSON is associated with the ELIZABETHAN period, the last part of the sixteenth century. Similarly, the novelist and playwright HENRY FIELDING is associated with the AUGUSTAN or eighteenth-century period.

71. **(c) In this place analogy, ARKANSAS and NEW MEXICO are interior states; FLORIDA and CALIFORNIA are related because they are coastal states.**

72. (c) ATONEMENT is compensation made for an offense against moral or religious law (a SIN). REPARATION is compensation made by a defeated nation for expenditures sustained by another nation as a result of WAR between the two nations.

73. (a) A PRIZEFIGHT is fought by SOLO contestants, one on each side; a BASKETBALL team is a QUINTET, five players on each side.

74. (b) In this object-to-action analogy, to clean a POT thoroughly you need to SCOUR it; to clean a PIPE thoroughly you need to REAM it.

75. (a) MEMORY, DENIM and WALLPAPER are all related because of a common characteristic. They all tend to fade. An ECHO also fades.

76. (b) In this association analogy, a SWORD is a symbol of warfare, associated with HANNIBAL, a great soldier; a CADUCEUS is a symbol for medicine and should be related to HIPPOCRATES, a famous physician.

77. (c) RADAR and LASER are related as acronyms; DEPT. and ACCT. are related as abbreviations.

78. (c) PALEONTOLOGY is concerned with the study of FOSSILS; EPISTEMOLOGY is concerned with the study of KNOWLEDGE.

79. (d) In this part-to-part analogy, a FIFE is used with a DRUM to make up a marching corps; a FLINT is used with STEEL to produce a fire.

80. (d) The correspondence is one of object to action. One can BLINK an EYE, and one can TOSS a CABER, a large pole which is thrown as a feat of strength in a Scottish sport.

81. (d) ARISTOTLE was a follower of PLATO; JUNG was a follower of FREUD.

82. (d) This analogy is one of worker to the article created. A LEXICOGRAPHER compiles a DICTIONARY; a WAINWRIGHT makes a WAGON.

83. (c) In this non-semantic analogy, the relationship is between common prefixes. RETIRE and REPRISE both begin with the prefix *re*; PROFILE and PROGRAM both have the prefix *pro*.

84. (b) A CONCERT in which there is singing without musical accompaniment is A CAPELLA; a dramatic PERFORMANCE in which there is no dialogue is a PANTOMIME.

85. (d) A SENTRY guards a GARRISON; a sheep DOG guards a FLOCK.

86. (d) PORTUGAL is part of the peninsula of IBERIA; a TOOTH is part of a COMB.

87. (d) A YARD (three feet) is half as long as a FATHOM (six feet). In a given circle, the RADIUS is half as long as the DIAMETER.

88. (c) EMINENT and LOWLY are antonyms; an antonym for FREQUENT is RARE.

89. (a) In this product-source analogy, FILIGREE is delicate ornamental openwork made of METAL; LACE is delicate open-work fabric made from THREAD.

90. (a) CONCAVE means curving inward whereas CONVEX means curving outward. INTAGLIO is incised carving. It relates, therefore, to CONCAVE. A CAMEO, which is carved in relief, corresponds to CONVEX.

91. (d) The MEZZANINE is located directly below the SECOND BALCONY; just as the ABDOMEN is located below the THORAX.

92. (c) BULBOUS, which means rotund or heavy, is the opposite of GAUNT, which means thin. An antonym for CONTUMACIOUS, meaning disobedient or rebellious, is TRACTABLE, meaning docile or yielding.

93. (a) A GLACIER, MOLASSES and a TORTOISE are all related because they move slowly. Among the choices only a DIRGE is also slow-moving.

94. (b) In this action-to-object analogy, one may FORD a STREAM and one can FOLD a HAND in cards.

95. (b) Because CHOPIN did not compose PARSIFAL, to complete the analogy, you must select what VERDI did not compose. The correct choice is FIDELIO.

96. (d) A SUBSTITUTE is used to replace someone on a TEAM; an UNDERSTUDY is used to replace someone in a CAST.

97. (c) PORT and STARBOARD are opposite sides of a ship; the HEADLIGHTS and the TRUNK are at opposite ends of an automobile.

98. (c) In this place analogy, YORKTOWN was the site of a major battle in the

Revolutionary War; VICKSBURG was the site of a major battle in the Civil War. Because CONCORD was also a site of a Revolutionary War battle, to complete the analogy, another site for a Civil War battle must be found. ANTIETAM is the correct choice.

99. (d) The relationship is an eight-to-one ratio, since an OCTAVE is a group of eight and MONOTHEISM is the belief in one God. A QUART consists of eight GILLS.

100. (d) Since EFFERVESCENT, meaning exuberant, and EFFETE, meaning exhausted, are opposites, the task is to find a contrast for ROOSTER. A rooster is synonymous with morning, whereas an OWL is a night bird.

ANSWER SHEET FOR
MILLER ANALOGIES SAMPLE TEST IV

1 Ⓐ Ⓑ Ⓒ Ⓓ	26 Ⓐ Ⓑ Ⓒ Ⓓ	51 Ⓐ Ⓑ Ⓒ Ⓓ	76 Ⓐ Ⓑ Ⓒ Ⓓ
2 Ⓐ Ⓑ Ⓒ Ⓓ	27 Ⓐ Ⓑ Ⓒ Ⓓ	52 Ⓐ Ⓑ Ⓒ Ⓓ	77 Ⓐ Ⓑ Ⓒ Ⓓ
3 Ⓐ Ⓑ Ⓒ Ⓓ	28 Ⓐ Ⓑ Ⓒ Ⓓ	53 Ⓐ Ⓑ Ⓒ Ⓓ	78 Ⓐ Ⓑ Ⓒ Ⓓ
4 Ⓐ Ⓑ Ⓒ Ⓓ	29 Ⓐ Ⓑ Ⓒ Ⓓ	54 Ⓐ Ⓑ Ⓒ Ⓓ	79 Ⓐ Ⓑ Ⓒ Ⓓ
5 Ⓐ Ⓑ Ⓒ Ⓓ	30 Ⓐ Ⓑ Ⓒ Ⓓ	55 Ⓐ Ⓑ Ⓒ Ⓓ	80 Ⓐ Ⓑ Ⓒ Ⓓ
6 Ⓐ Ⓑ Ⓒ Ⓓ	31 Ⓐ Ⓑ Ⓒ Ⓓ	56 Ⓐ Ⓑ Ⓒ Ⓓ	81 Ⓐ Ⓑ Ⓒ Ⓓ
7 Ⓐ Ⓑ Ⓒ Ⓓ	32 Ⓐ Ⓑ Ⓒ Ⓓ	57 Ⓐ Ⓑ Ⓒ Ⓓ	82 Ⓐ Ⓑ Ⓒ Ⓓ
8 Ⓐ Ⓑ Ⓒ Ⓓ	33 Ⓐ Ⓑ Ⓒ Ⓓ	58 Ⓐ Ⓑ Ⓒ Ⓓ	83 Ⓐ Ⓑ Ⓒ Ⓓ
9 Ⓐ Ⓑ Ⓒ Ⓓ	34 Ⓐ Ⓑ Ⓒ Ⓓ	59 Ⓐ Ⓑ Ⓒ Ⓓ	84 Ⓐ Ⓑ Ⓒ Ⓓ
10 Ⓐ Ⓑ Ⓒ Ⓓ	35 Ⓐ Ⓑ Ⓒ Ⓓ	60 Ⓐ Ⓑ Ⓒ Ⓓ	85 Ⓐ Ⓑ Ⓒ Ⓓ
11 Ⓐ Ⓑ Ⓒ Ⓓ	36 Ⓐ Ⓑ Ⓒ Ⓓ	61 Ⓐ Ⓑ Ⓒ Ⓓ	86 Ⓐ Ⓑ Ⓒ Ⓓ
12 Ⓐ Ⓑ Ⓒ Ⓓ	37 Ⓐ Ⓑ Ⓒ Ⓓ	62 Ⓐ Ⓑ Ⓒ Ⓓ	87 Ⓐ Ⓑ Ⓒ Ⓓ
13 Ⓐ Ⓑ Ⓒ Ⓓ	38 Ⓐ Ⓑ Ⓒ Ⓓ	63 Ⓐ Ⓑ Ⓒ Ⓓ	88 Ⓐ Ⓑ Ⓒ Ⓓ
14 Ⓐ Ⓑ Ⓒ Ⓓ	39 Ⓐ Ⓑ Ⓒ Ⓓ	64 Ⓐ Ⓑ Ⓒ Ⓓ	89 Ⓐ Ⓑ Ⓒ Ⓓ
15 Ⓐ Ⓑ Ⓒ Ⓓ	40 Ⓐ Ⓑ Ⓒ Ⓓ	65 Ⓐ Ⓑ Ⓒ Ⓓ	90 Ⓐ Ⓑ Ⓒ Ⓓ
16 Ⓐ Ⓑ Ⓒ Ⓓ	41 Ⓐ Ⓑ Ⓒ Ⓓ	66 Ⓐ Ⓑ Ⓒ Ⓓ	91 Ⓐ Ⓑ Ⓒ Ⓓ
17 Ⓐ Ⓑ Ⓒ Ⓓ	42 Ⓐ Ⓑ Ⓒ Ⓓ	67 Ⓐ Ⓑ Ⓒ Ⓓ	92 Ⓐ Ⓑ Ⓒ Ⓓ
18 Ⓐ Ⓑ Ⓒ Ⓓ	43 Ⓐ Ⓑ Ⓒ Ⓓ	68 Ⓐ Ⓑ Ⓒ Ⓓ	93 Ⓐ Ⓑ Ⓒ Ⓓ
19 Ⓐ Ⓑ Ⓒ Ⓓ	44 Ⓐ Ⓑ Ⓒ Ⓓ	69 Ⓐ Ⓑ Ⓒ Ⓓ	94 Ⓐ Ⓑ Ⓒ Ⓓ
20 Ⓐ Ⓑ Ⓒ Ⓓ	45 Ⓐ Ⓑ Ⓒ Ⓓ	70 Ⓐ Ⓑ Ⓒ Ⓓ	95 Ⓐ Ⓑ Ⓒ Ⓓ
21 Ⓐ Ⓑ Ⓒ Ⓓ	46 Ⓐ Ⓑ Ⓒ Ⓓ	71 Ⓐ Ⓑ Ⓒ Ⓓ	96 Ⓐ Ⓑ Ⓒ Ⓓ
22 Ⓐ Ⓑ Ⓒ Ⓓ	47 Ⓐ Ⓑ Ⓒ Ⓓ	72 Ⓐ Ⓑ Ⓒ Ⓓ	97 Ⓐ Ⓑ Ⓒ Ⓓ
23 Ⓐ Ⓑ Ⓒ Ⓓ	48 Ⓐ Ⓑ Ⓒ Ⓓ	73 Ⓐ Ⓑ Ⓒ Ⓓ	98 Ⓐ Ⓑ Ⓒ Ⓓ
24 Ⓐ Ⓑ Ⓒ Ⓓ	49 Ⓐ Ⓑ Ⓒ Ⓓ	74 Ⓐ Ⓑ Ⓒ Ⓓ	99 Ⓐ Ⓑ Ⓒ Ⓓ
25 Ⓐ Ⓑ Ⓒ Ⓓ	50 Ⓐ Ⓑ Ⓒ Ⓓ	75 Ⓐ Ⓑ Ⓒ Ⓓ	100 Ⓐ Ⓑ Ⓒ Ⓓ

MILLER ANALOGIES SAMPLE TEST IV

Directions: Each of these test questions consists of three CAPI-
TALIZED words and four lettered words enclosed in parentheses.
Two of the capitalized words are related in some way. Find the two
related words and establish the nature of the relationship. Then study
the four words lettered a, b, c and d. Select the one lettered word
which is related to the remaining capitalized word in the same way
that the first two capitalized words are related. Mark the Answer
Sheet for the letter preceding the word you select.

1. NEEDLE : (a. thread, b. pen, c. eye, d. hole) :: GLOBE : ORANGE

2. ARCHIPELAGO : ISLAND :: GALAXY : (a. universe, b. space, c. star,
   d. Milky Way)

3. DUCTILE : (a. malleable, b. adamant, c. regal, d. channel) :: LATENT :
   COVERT

4. NEWSPRINT : (a. paper, b. linotype, c. newsstand, d. tree) :: STEEL :
   ORE

5. EXPERIMENTATION : MATRICULATION :: DISCOVERY :
   (a. mothering, b. molding, c. learning, d. wedding)

6. FORKED : (a. bend, b. cull, c. sharp, d. baked) :: LISP : RASPBERRY

7. (a. thunder, b. lightning, c. melodious, d. cloudy) : LOUD :: CONCERT :
   ONCE

8. RIFLE : MISSILE :: LANCE : (a. bayonet, b. bomb, c. pistol, d. catapult)

9. 121 : 12 :: (a. 101, b. 141, c. 100, d. 125) : 11

10. CLAWING : (a. scratching, b. devouring, c. crippling, d. pawing) ::
    VIOLENCE : BRASHNESS

11. (a. Bartók, b. Mozart, c. Fauré, d. Beethoven) : WAGNER :: TCHAIKOV-
    SKY : PROKOFIEV

12. (a. grind, b. thresh, c. harvest, d. grow) : WHEAT :: DISTILL : WATER

95

13. BRAGGADOCIO : RETICENCE :: MISERLINESS : (a. profligacy, b. ecstasy, c. obloquy, d. falsity)

14. (a. mined, b. minor, c. miner, d. canvas) : DENIM :: GULP : PLUG

15. SANDHURST : ENGLAND :: (a. Harvard, b. Pittsburgh, c. West Point, d. M.I.T.) : UNITED STATES

16. AURICLE : VENTRICLE :: (a. sinus, b. epiglottis, c. thalamus, d. esophagus) : CEREBELLUM

17. (a. trees, b. circus, c. merry-go-round, d. scooter) : STILTS :: BUS : AUDITORIUM

18. PARIS : (a. London, b. Priam, c. Achilles, d. Helen) :: ACHILLES : HECTOR

19. GENEROUS : LAVISH :: TIMOROUS : (a. tumid, b. craven, c. courageous, d. foolhardy)

20. MECCA : BENARES :: MOSLEM : (a. Islam, b. India, c. Hindu, d. Buddhist)

21. POLO : ROLLS :: (a. mansion, b. mallet, c. race, d. swimming) : YACHT

22. (a. barber, b. bristle, c. comb, d. stroke) : BRUSH :: CRUISER : FLEET

23. HUDSON : BUICK :: PACKARD : (a. Stutz, b. Locomobile, c. Maxwell, d. Oldsmobile)

24. IMBROGLIO : SYMMETRY :: (a. dentures, b. savory, c. distasteful, d. cavernous) : TOOTHSOME

25. (a. Galen, b. Magyar, c. Bede, d. Pericles) : LUKE :: SCHWEITZER :: SALK

26. ASSAYER : ORE :: TRENCHERMAN : (a. ditch, b. food, c. dikes, d. security)

27. RECEIVE : DIARRHEA :: PENNICILIN : (a. figure, b. classification, c. batallion, d. geometry)

28. (a. lunch, b. meal, c. breakfast, d. brunch) : SUPPER :: SMOG : HAZE

29. APPRAISAL : REVENUE :: (a. defrosting, b. clear, c. hiding, d. sun) : VISIBILITY

30. F : X :: 1 : (a. 4, b. 8, c. 2, d. 6)

31. RUPEE : (a. shah, b. guilder, c. rizal, d. krone) :: INDIA : NETHERLANDS

32. (a. servile, b. kowtow, c. refractory, d. inhibited) : OBSEQUIOUS :: IMPRECATORY : EULOGISTIC

33. BLUE : ORANGE :: (a. indigo, b. yellow, c. purple, d. red) : GREEN

34. CHEETAH : SPEED :: (a. blade, b. cleavage, c. bird, d. incision) : KEENNESS

35. (a. hock, b. jockey, c. stable, d. hand) : HORSE :: TONGUE : BELL

36. EPILOGUE : NOVEL :: (a. cheers, b. curtain call, c. performance, d. introduction) : APPLAUSE

37. (a. Nantucket, b. Puerto Rico, c. Hawaii, d. Long Island) : UNITED STATES :: TASMANIA : AUSTRALIA

38. ANCHISES : (a. Troilus, b. Achilles, c. Ajax, d. Aeneas) :: JOCASTA : OEDIPUS

39. LEES : DREGS :: SYBARITIC : (a. sensual, b. moderate, c. cultish, d. servile)

40. DEVIL : LIVED :: GOLF : (a. club, b. polo, c. whip, d. flog)

41. MAP : (a. explorer, b. geography, c. legend, d. atlas) :: TEXT : FOOTNOTE

42. (a. clock, b. watch, c. time, d. hour) : TELL :: GUM : CHEW

43. YANKEE DOODLE : DUSTER :: PILLOW : (a. coop, b. macaroni, c. blanket, d. broom)

44. COOPER : (a. lithographer, b. cartographer, c. photographer, d. biographer) :: BARREL : MAP

45. PUPA : (a. tadpole, d. larva, c. cocoon, d. bumblebee) :: FETUS : CHILD

46. DEALING : STOCK EXCHANGE :: (a. preserving. b. selling, c. buying, d. copying) : LANDMARK

47. UPRISING : (a. revolution, b. settlement, c. quarrel, d. disquiet) :: FIB : LIE

48. (a. Crete, b. Malta, c. Sicily, d. Corsica) : SARDINIA :: BOLIVIA : ARGENTINA

49. EVIL : EXORCISE :: BREAD : (a. carbohydrate, b. break, c. sandwich, d. shred)

50. COWARD : (a. loser, b. lily-livered, c. hero, d. villain) :: YOLK : ALBUMEN

51. (a. humid, b. speedy, c. piquant, d. moist) : VAPID :: OBDURATE : COMPASSIONATE

52. CUCUMBER : WATERMELON :: CANTALOUPE : (a. squash, b. radish, c. cherry, d. plum)

53. (a. head, b. nose, c. ear, d. limbs) : MAN :: STRINGS : VIOLIN

54. ILLNESS : (a. debility, b. hospital, c. doctor, d. panacea) :: VIBRA-TION : SOUND

55. VERDUN : DUNKIRK :: YPRES : (a. Bateau Woods, b. El Alamein, c. San Juan Hill, d. Marne)

56. (a. gain, b. reward, c. loot, d. profit) : ROBBERY :: REVENGE : VENDETTA

57. ANALYSIS : FREUD :: (a. manipulation, b. illness, c. sex, d. stimulation) : OSTEOPATHY

58. CLAUSTROPHOBIA : CLOSETS :: AGORAPHOBIA : (a. ships, b. sheep, c. plants, d. plains)

59. SEARCH : FIND :: FIGHT : (a. win, b. lose, c. seek, d. contend)

60. (a. sympathy, b. encouragement, c. blasphemy, d. oblivion) : FRACAS :: APHRODITE : MARS

61. H : S :: (a. M, b. L, c. I, d. P) : W

62. HASTILY : DESPONDENTLY :: CIRCUMSPECTLY : (a. quick, b. circuit, c. rate, d. slowly)

63. BOXER : TABBY :: LABRADOR : (a. fighter, b. poodle, c. calico, d. nanny)

64. CROESUS : (a. boat, b. wealth, c. pleats, d. loyalty) :: ODYSSEUS : CRAFT

65. LUCERNE : MICHIGAN :: GENEVA : (a. United States, b. Victoria, c. Okeechobee, d. Switzerland)

66. (a. tally, b. game, c. concert, d. run) : SCORE :: PLAY : SCRIPT

67. HERRING : (a. salt, b. sea, c. egg, d. ham) :: CIGARETTE : VOLCANO

68. BAT : INSECT :: (a. lizard, b. fire, c. knight, d. maiden) : DRAGON

69. CLEAVE : REND :: SALIENT : (a. contrite, b. unknown, c. inconspicuous, d. secure)

70. PARTRIDGE : RABBIT :: (a. quail, b. pen, c. birds, d. covey) : WARREN

71. LAPIDARY : (a. ruby, b. wood, c. lick, d. food) :: SCULPTOR : ALABASTER

72. WOOF : FILE :: WARP : (a. grade, b. rank, c. fold, d. twist)

73. SMILE : (a. rile, b. style, c. while, d. tile) :: SEEMS : DREAMS

74. FORSOOK : DRANK :: FROZEN : (a. swum, b. wrote, c. sang, d. chose)

75. SANDAL : BOOT :: (a. hammer, b. hatchet, c. shoemaker, d. blade) : AX

76. HORSE : (a. man, b. goat, c. archer, d. bull) :: CENTAUR : SATYR

77. (a. anode, b. bird, c. purchase, d. battery) : CELL :: ARROW : SHAFT

78. FELONY : MISDEMEANOR :: SIN : (a. piccalilli, b. picayune, c. peccadillo, d. picador)

79. NOVEMBER : APRIL :: (a. May, b. June, c. July, d. August) : SEPTEMBER

80. ENTRY : YIELD :: INVITE : (a. halibut, b. jewelry, c. binder, d. esteem)

81. WASTEFUL : (a. parsimonious, b. neglectful, c. vast, d. prodigal) :: DISINTERESTED : IMPARTIAL

82. SCHOONER : ZIGGURAT :: CRUISER : (a. cutter, b. campanile, c. viking, d. tug)

83. (a. pine, b. cedar, c. ash, d. willow) : OAK :: MOURNFUL : STURDY

84. ADVISE : EXHORT :: (a. force, b. tempt, c. prohibit, d. prevent) : ENTICE

85. STEEL : WELD :: LIPS : (a. frown, b. purse, c. fold, d. smirk)

86. TESTIMONY : (a. confession, b. judge, c. witness, d. trial) :: BIOGRAPHY : AUTOBIOGRAPHY

87. STRATUM : SYLLABUS :: (a. strati, b. stratums, c. stratus, d. strata) : SYLLABI

88. LAMB : DEER :: (a. rabbit, b. peacock, c. horse, d. pig) : LION

89. VELOCITY : (a. wind, b. earth, c. vibration, d. destruction) :: BEAUFORT : RICHTER

90. (a. distance, b. program, c. station, d. tube) : TELEVISION :: LEADER : ANARCHY

91. TATTOO : VESPERS :: (a. painting, b. needle, c. revelry, d. reveille) : MATINS

92. PROSTRATE : (a. dazzling, b. stealing, c. yielding, d. dreaming) :: SUPINE : SLEEPING

93. MAHATMA GANDHI : WAR :: CARRY NATION : (a. suffrage, b. alcohol, c. temperance, d. employment)

94. 2/7 : (a. 1/16, b. 3/28, c. 3/21, d. 1/14) :: 4/7 : 1/7

95. (a. hydra, b. canary, c. albatross, d. condor) : VULTURE :: PHOENIX : EAGLE

96. TINE : FORK :: (a. car, b. gearshift, c. flange, d. wheelwright) : WHEEL

97. (a. tie, b. appearance, c. shoes, d. decoration) : ATTIRE :: WIT : COMMUNICATION

98. HUSK : (a. fat, b. chops, c. gristle, d. filet) :: GRAIN : MEAT

99. STARTLED : (a. interested, b. astounded, c. expected, d. unknown) :: WORK : TOIL

100. INEBRIOUS : (a. intoxicated, b. dull, c. sincere, d. abstemious) :: SPARTAN : GARRULOUS

ANSWER KEY FOR MILLER ANALOGIES SAMPLE TEST IV

1.	b	21.	a	41.	c	61.	b	81.	d
2.	c	22.	b	42.	c	62.	d	82.	b
3.	a	23.	d	43.	a	63.	c	83.	d
4.	d	24.	c	44.	b	64.	b	84.	b
5.	c	25.	a	45.	d	65.	c	85.	b
6.	c	26.	b	46.	a	66.	c	86.	a
7.	d	27.	c	47.	a	67.	d	87.	d
8.	d	28.	d	48.	d	68.	c	88.	b
9.	c	29.	a	49.	b	69.	c	89.	c
10.	a	30.	a	50.	c	70.	d	90.	a
11.	d	31.	b	51.	c	71.	a	91.	d
12.	b	32.	c	52.	a	72.	b	92.	c
13.	a	33.	d	53.	d	73.	b	93.	b
14.	a	34.	a	54.	a	74.	a	94.	d
15.	c	35.	a	55.	b	75.	b	95.	a
16.	c	36.	b	56.	c	76.	b	96.	c
17.	d	37.	c	57.	a	77.	d	97.	d
18.	c	38.	d	58.	d	78.	c	98.	c
19.	b	39.	a	59.	a	79.	b	99.	b
20.	c	40.	d	60.	a	80.	d	100.	d

EXPLANATORY ANSWERS FOR
MILLER ANALOGIES SAMPLE TEST IVI

1. (b) A GLOBE and an ORANGE are related because they are both round; a NEEDLE and a PEN are both pointed.

2. (c) This a whole-to-part analogy. An ARCHIPELAGO is made up of ISLANDs; a GALAXY is made up of STARs.

3. (a) LATENT and COVERT are synonyms meaning hidden or concealed. A synonym for DUCTILE, which means easily influenced or altered, is MALLEABLE.

4. (d) In this analogy the relationship is one of source to product. An indirect source of STEEL is ORE; an indirect source of NEWSPRINT is a TREE.

5. (c) In this purpose analogy, a purpose of EXPERIMENTATION is DISCOVERY; a purpose of MATRICULATION is learning.

6. (c) The correspondence is one of association. A LISP, a RASPBERRY (a jeering noise), and FORKED are all words associated with the tongue. Among the choices, only SHARP is also associated with the tongue.

7. (d) In this non-semantic analogy, the second, third, fourth and fifth letters of CLOUDY and CONCERT are LOUD and ONCE respectively.

8. (d) The relationship is one of new to old. A RIFLE and a MISSILE are modern weapons. A LANCE is a rifle's antiquated counterpart. The predecessor of a missile is a CATAPULT. Note that sword is also a more antiquated weapon, but it is less directly a counterpart of missile.

9. (c) In this mathematical analogy, $11 \times 11 = 121$, $11 + 1 = 12$; $10 \times 10 = 100$, $10 + 1 = 11$.

10. (a) This is an analogy of degree. VIOLENCE is an extreme degree of BRASHNESS; CLAWING is an extreme degree of SCRATCHING.

11. (d) TCHAIKOVSKY and PROKOFIEF are related because they both are composers from Russia; therefore WAGNER, who is a composer from GERMANY, must be paired with BEETHOVEN, another German composer, in order to complete the analogy.

12. (b) In this action-to-object analogy, you DISTILL WATER to remove unwanted substances from the refined water; similarly, you THRESH WHEAT to separate the grains from the unwanted chaff.

13. (a) BRAGGADOCIO, which means boastfulness, is opposite to RETICENCE; an antonym for MISERLINESS, which means stinginess, is PROFLIGACY, meaning reckless wastefulness.

14. (a) MINED spelled backwards is DENIM; PLUG spelled backwards is GULP.

15. (c) SANDHURST is a school in ENGLAND which trains future military officers; WEST POINT has the same function in the UNITED STATES.

16. (c) In this part-to-part analogy, an AURICLE and VENTRICLE are both parts of the heart; a CEREBELLUM and THALAMUS are parts of the brain.

17. (d) A BUS and an AUDITORIUM are related because they are intended to serve more than one person; STILTS and a SCOOTER are usually intended for one person alone.

18. (c) In Homer's *Iliad*, ACHILLES slew HECTOR, and later PARIS slew ACHILLES.

19. (b) A person who is extremely GENEROUS is LAVISH; a person who is extremely TIMOROUS is CRAVEN, or cowardly.

20. (c) In this place analogy, MECCA is the sacred city of the MOSLEMS; BENARES is the sacred city of the HINDUS.

21. (a) POLO, a ROLLS Royce, and a YACHT are all things associated with rich people. Among the choices, MANSION is also associated with the wealthy.

22. (b) In this analogy of a part to a whole, a BRISTLE is part of a BRUSH; a CRUISER is part of a FLEET.

23. (d) HUDSON and PACKARD are names of cars that are no longer made; BUICK and OLDSMOBILE are names of popular current cars.

24. (c) IMBROGLIO, which means disorder, is opposite in meaning to SYMMETRY. An antonym for TOOTHSOME, which means palatable, is DISTASTEFUL.

25. (a) GALEN, LUKE, SCHWEITZER and SALK are all related as physicians.

26. (b) In this analogy of association, an ASSAYER's job is to analyze ORE; a TRENCHERMAN's avocation is the enjoyment of FOOD.

27. (c) RECEIVE and DIARRHEA are both spelled correctly. PENNI-CILIN, which is spelled incorrectly, must therefore be paired with BATALLION, which is also spelled incorrectly.

28. (d) There is a two-to-one relationship in this analogy since BRUNCH combines two meals, breakfast and lunch, and SUPPER is just one meal. Similarly, SMOG is a combination of two atmospheric conditions, smoke and fog, and HAZE is one atmospheric condition.

29. (a) This is a purpose analogy. The purpose of the APPRAISAL of a house is to gain tax REVENUE; the purpose of DEFROSTING a windshield is to increase VISIBILITY. Note that the sun is a cause of visibility, not the purpose of it.

30. (a) The correspondence is mathematical. F is the sixth letter of the alphabet and X is the twenty-fourth. Their ratio is 1 : 4.

31. (b) The RUPEE is the basic unit of currency in INDIA. The basic unit of currency in the NETHERLANDS is the GUILDER.

32. (c) IMPRECATORY, which means damning, is opposite to EULO-GISTIC, meaning full of praise. Similarly, an antonym of OBSEQUI-OUS, meaning compliant, is REFRACTORY, which means unruly.

33. (d) BLUE and ORANGE are related as complementary colors; RED and GREEN are also complementary colors.

34. (a) In this characteristic analogy, a CHEETAH is known for its SPEED; a BLADE is proverbial for its KEENNESS.

35. (a) The correspondence is one of part to whole. A HOCK is part of a HORSE, the joint of the hind leg; a TONGUE is part of a BELL.

36. (b) In this sequence analogy, an EPILOGUE follows the main action of a NOVEL. A CURTAIN CALL follows APPLAUSE in a performance.

37. (c) TASMANIA is an island state of AUSTRALIA; HAWAII is an island state of the UNITED STATES.

38. (d) JOCASTA was the mother of OEDIPUS; ANCHISES was the father of AENEAS.

39. (a) LEES is a synonym for DREGS. Similarly, a synonym for SYBARITIC, devoted to pleasure of luxury, is SENSUAL.

40. (d) In this non-semantic analogy, DEVIL is LIVED spelled backwards; GOLF is FLOG spelled backwards.

41. (c) A FOOTNOTE is an explanatory reference in a TEXT; a LEGEND is an explanatory list of the symbols used on a MAP.

42. (c) In this action-to-object analogy, one can TELL TIME and one can CHEW GUM.

43. (a) YANKEE DOODLE, a DUSTER and a PILLOW are related because each is associated with feathers. To complete the analogy, you must select another term associated with feathers, and a chicken COOP is the correct choice.

44. (b) The correspondence is one of worker to the thing created. A COOPER makes a BARREL; a CARTOGRAPHER makes a MAP.

45. (d) In this classification analogy, the PUPA is the last stage of development before the birth of a BUMBLEBEE; the FETUS is the last stage of development before the birth of a CHILD.

46. (a) The correspondence is one of action to situation. DEALING is an activity related to the STOCK EXCHANGE. PRESERVING is a typical activity associated with a LANDMARK.

47. (a) In this analogy of degree, a FIB is not quite telling a LIE; an UPRISING may not quite be a REVOLUTION.

48. (d) The relationship is one of place. BOLIVA is a country directly north of ARGENTINA. CORSICA is an island located directly north of the island of SARDINIA.

49. (b) The correspondence is one of object to action. One may EXORCISE EVIL; one may BREAK BREAD.

50. (c) The YOLK is the yellow part of an egg and the ALBUMEN is part of the egg white. A COWARD is associated with the color yellow; a HERO is associated with the color white.

51. (c) OBDURATE, meaning hardened in feelings, and COMPASSION-ATE, meaning sympathetic to the distress of others, are antonyms. PIQUANT, meaning pungent or savory, and VAPID, meaning insipid or flat, are also antonyms.

52. (a) CUCUMBER, WATERMELON, CANTALOUPE, and SQUASH are all related because they have many seeds and grow on vines.

53. (d) In this part-to-whole analogy, a VIOLIN has four STRINGS. The task, therefore, is to determine what MAN has four of, and the correct answer is LIMBS.

54. (a) The correspondence is one of cause and effect. ILLNESS causes DEBILITY; VIBRATION causes SOUND.

55. (b) VERDUN and YPRES were battles fought in World War I; DUNKIRK and EL ALAMEIN were famous battles of World War II.

56. (c) REVENGE is the object of a VENDETTA; LOOT is the object of a ROBBERY. Gain or profit might also be objects of robbery, but loot is a more specific and characteristic object.

57. (a) FREUD attempted to relieve mental disorders through ANALYSIS; OSTEOPATHY attempts to relieve physical disorders through MANIPU-LATION of affected parts.

58. (d) A person suffering from CLAUSTROPHOBIA (a fear of closed spaces) would fear CLOSETS; a person suffering from AGORAPHOBIA (fear of open spaces) would fear PLAINS.

59. (a) A positive result of a SEARCH is to FIND what you are looking for; a positive result of a FIGHT is to WIN.

60. (a) In mythology, MARS, as the god of war, would encourage a FRACAS; as the goddess of love, APHRODITE would encourage SYMPATHY.

61. (b) In this sequence analogy, the difference between H, the eighth letter in the alphabet, and S, the nineteenth, is eleven. The letter with the same relation to W, the twenty-third letter, is L, the twelfth letter in the alphabet.

62. (d) The correspondence here is grammatical. HASTILY, DESPON-DENTLY and CIRCUMSPECTLY are all related as adverbs. Among the choices only SLOWLY is also an adverb.

63. (c) A BOXER is a type of dog; a TABBY is a kind of cat. Because a LABRADOR is another breed of dog, the task is to select another type of cat, CALICO.

64. (b) In this characteristic analogy, CROESUS was known for his great WEALTH; ODYSSEUS was known for his great CRAFT.

65. (c) In this place analogy, Lake LUCERNE and Lake GENEVA are in Switzerland; Lake MICHIGAN and Lake OKEECHOBEE are in the United States.

66. (c) The SCRIPT is the written text of a PLAY; the SCORE is the written version of the music to be played at a CONCERT.

67. (d) The given words HERRING, CIGARETTE, and VOLCANO are related because each is associated with smoke. Among the answer choices, only HAM is also associated with smoke.

68. (c) A BAT is a natural foe of an INSECT; a KNIGHT is the fictional foe of a DRAGON.

69. (c) CLEAVE, meaning to adhere firmly, and REND, meaning to tear apart violently, are opposites. An opposite for SALIENT, meaning prominent, is INCONSPICUOUS, meaning not readily noticeable.

70. (d) RABBITs congregate in a WARREN; PARTRIDGEs congregate in a COVEY.

71. (a) The relationship is one of worker to his material. A LAPIDARY (an engraver of precious stones) may work with a RUBY; a SCULPTOR may work with ALABASTER.

72. (b) The correspondence is one of association. We speak of WARP and WOOF and also of RANK and FILE.

73. (b) In this non-semantic rhyming analogy, SEEMS and DREAMS rhyme, but the rhyming vowels are spelled differently (*ee* and *ea*); therefore, the task is to pick a word that rhymes with SMILE but has a different letter for its rhyming vowel. STYLE is the correct choice.

74. (a) In this grammatical analogy, FORSOOK and DRANK are simple past tenses; FROZEN and SWUM are past participles.

75. (b) This relationship is one of degree. A SANDAL is a lighter version of footwear than a BOOT; a HATCHET is a smaller version of a sharp-edged instrument than an AX.

76. (b) In this mythological analogy, a CENTAUR is half HORSE, half man; a SATYR is half GOAT, half man.

77. (d) The correspondence is one of whole to part. A CELL is part of a BATTERY; a SHAFT is part of an ARROW.

78. (c) In this degree analogy, a FELONY is a more serious offense than a MISDEMEANOR; similarly, a SIN is a more serious offense than a PECCADILLO (a slight offense).

79. (b) In the well-known adage, thirty days hath SEPTEMBER, APRIL, JUNE, and NOVEMBER.

80. (d) ENTRY ends with a *y*, YIELD begins with a *y*; INVITE ends with an *e*, ESTEEM begins with an *e*.

81. (d) DISINTERESTED is a synonym for IMPARTIAL; a synonym for WASTEFUL is PRODIGAL.

82. (b) A SCHOONER and a CRUISER are both types of ships. A ZIGGURAT and a CAMPANILE are both types of towers.

83. (d) In this characteristic analogy, we speak of the mighty (STURDY) OAK and the weeping (MOURNFUL) WILLOW.

84. (b) The relationship is one of degree. EXHORT means to urge on, which is a stronger degree of ADVISE; ENTICE is a stronger degree of TEMPT.

85. (b) In this action-to-object analogy, you WELD two pieces of STEEL to join or hold them together; you PURSE your LIPS by holding or pressing them together.

86. (a) TESTIMONY is a statement about someone else, a CONFESSION is a statement about oneself; a BIOGRAPHY is written history of another person's life; an AUTOBIOGRAPHY is written history of one's own life.

87. (d) The relationship in this analogy is grammatical. The plural of SYLLABUS is SYLLABI; the plural of STRATUM is STRATA.

88. (b) A LAMB and a DEER are related because they are both considered timid; a PEACOCK and a LION are related because they are both considered proud.

89. (c) The BEAUFORT Scale (invented by Sir Francis Beaufort) indicates VELOCITY of the wind in numbers from 0 to 12. The RICHTER Scale (named after Charles Richter) indicates the magnitude of a seismic VIBRATION or earthquake.

90. (a) The Greek root *tele* in TELEVISION means DISTANCE; the Greek root *arch* in ANARCHY means LEADER.

91. (d) A TATTOO is an evening military signal, and VESPERS are evening prayers; REVEILLE is a morning military signal, and MATINS are morning prayers.

92. (c) In this situation-to-action analogy, a person who is PROSTRATE is in a position for YIELDING; a person who is SUPINE is in a position for SLEEPING.

93. (b) MAHATMA GANDHI was opposed to all forms of violence including WAR as CARRY NATION was opposed to the use of any kind of ALCOHOL.

94. (d) In this mathematical analogy, 1/4 of 4/7 is 1/7; 1/4 of 2/7 is 1/14.

95. (a) The relationship is one of real to imaginary. A PHOENIX is an imaginary bird and an EAGLE is an actual bird. Similarly, a HYDRA is imaginary and a VULTURE is real.

96. (c) A TINE is part of a FORK; a FLANGE is part of a WHEEL.

97. (d) One's ATTIRE is brightened with some DECORATION; one's COMMUNICATION is brightened with WIT.

98. (c) In this analogy the relationship is one of discardable to usable. The HUSK is the discardable part of GRAIN; GRISTLE is the discardable part of MEAT. Note that fat may be discarded or not.

99. (b) The correspondence is one of degree. WORK is a milder form of TOIL; STARTLED is a milder form of ASTOUNDED.

100. (d) SPARTAN, meaning terse in speech, is the opposite of GARRULOUS. INEBRIOUS, which means drunken, is the opposite of ABSTEMIOUS, or temperate.

ANSWER SHEET FOR
MILLER ANALOGIES SAMPLE TEST V

1 Ⓐ Ⓑ Ⓒ Ⓓ	26 Ⓐ Ⓑ Ⓒ Ⓓ	51 Ⓐ Ⓑ Ⓒ Ⓓ	76 Ⓐ Ⓑ Ⓒ Ⓓ
2 Ⓐ Ⓑ Ⓒ Ⓓ	27 Ⓐ Ⓑ Ⓒ Ⓓ	52 Ⓐ Ⓑ Ⓒ Ⓓ	77 Ⓐ Ⓑ Ⓒ Ⓓ
3 Ⓐ Ⓑ Ⓒ Ⓓ	28 Ⓐ Ⓑ Ⓒ Ⓓ	53 Ⓐ Ⓑ Ⓒ Ⓓ	78 Ⓐ Ⓑ Ⓒ Ⓓ
4 Ⓐ Ⓑ Ⓒ Ⓓ	29 Ⓐ Ⓑ Ⓒ Ⓓ	54 Ⓐ Ⓑ Ⓒ Ⓓ	79 Ⓐ Ⓑ Ⓒ Ⓓ
5 Ⓐ Ⓑ Ⓒ Ⓓ	30 Ⓐ Ⓑ Ⓒ Ⓓ	55 Ⓐ Ⓑ Ⓒ Ⓓ	80 Ⓐ Ⓑ Ⓒ Ⓓ
6 Ⓐ Ⓑ Ⓒ Ⓓ	31 Ⓐ Ⓑ Ⓒ Ⓓ	56 Ⓐ Ⓑ Ⓒ Ⓓ	81 Ⓐ Ⓑ Ⓒ Ⓓ
7 Ⓐ Ⓑ Ⓒ Ⓓ	32 Ⓐ Ⓑ Ⓒ Ⓓ	57 Ⓐ Ⓑ Ⓒ Ⓓ	82 Ⓐ Ⓑ Ⓒ Ⓓ
8 Ⓐ Ⓑ Ⓒ Ⓓ	33 Ⓐ Ⓑ Ⓒ Ⓓ	58 Ⓐ Ⓑ Ⓒ Ⓓ	83 Ⓐ Ⓑ Ⓒ Ⓓ
9 Ⓐ Ⓑ Ⓒ Ⓓ	34 Ⓐ Ⓑ Ⓒ Ⓓ	59 Ⓐ Ⓑ Ⓒ Ⓓ	84 Ⓐ Ⓑ Ⓒ Ⓓ
10 Ⓐ Ⓑ Ⓒ Ⓓ	35 Ⓐ Ⓑ Ⓒ Ⓓ	60 Ⓐ Ⓑ Ⓒ Ⓓ	85 Ⓐ Ⓑ Ⓒ Ⓓ
11 Ⓐ Ⓑ Ⓒ Ⓓ	36 Ⓐ Ⓑ Ⓒ Ⓓ	61 Ⓐ Ⓑ Ⓒ Ⓓ	86 Ⓐ Ⓑ Ⓒ Ⓓ
12 Ⓐ Ⓑ Ⓒ Ⓓ	37 Ⓐ Ⓑ Ⓒ Ⓓ	62 Ⓐ Ⓑ Ⓒ Ⓓ	87 Ⓐ Ⓑ Ⓒ Ⓓ
13 Ⓐ Ⓑ Ⓒ Ⓓ	38 Ⓐ Ⓑ Ⓒ Ⓓ	63 Ⓐ Ⓑ Ⓒ Ⓓ	88 Ⓐ Ⓑ Ⓒ Ⓓ
14 Ⓐ Ⓑ Ⓒ Ⓓ	39 Ⓐ Ⓑ Ⓒ Ⓓ	64 Ⓐ Ⓑ Ⓒ Ⓓ	89 Ⓐ Ⓑ Ⓒ Ⓓ
15 Ⓐ Ⓑ Ⓒ Ⓓ	40 Ⓐ Ⓑ Ⓒ Ⓓ	65 Ⓐ Ⓑ Ⓒ Ⓓ	90 Ⓐ Ⓑ Ⓒ Ⓓ
16 Ⓐ Ⓑ Ⓒ Ⓓ	41 Ⓐ Ⓑ Ⓒ Ⓓ	66 Ⓐ Ⓑ Ⓒ Ⓓ	91 Ⓐ Ⓑ Ⓒ Ⓓ
17 Ⓐ Ⓑ Ⓒ Ⓓ	42 Ⓐ Ⓑ Ⓒ Ⓓ	67 Ⓐ Ⓑ Ⓒ Ⓓ	92 Ⓐ Ⓑ Ⓒ Ⓓ
18 Ⓐ Ⓑ Ⓒ Ⓓ	43 Ⓐ Ⓑ Ⓒ Ⓓ	68 Ⓐ Ⓑ Ⓒ Ⓓ	93 Ⓐ Ⓑ Ⓒ Ⓓ
19 Ⓐ Ⓑ Ⓒ Ⓓ	44 Ⓐ Ⓑ Ⓒ Ⓓ	69 Ⓐ Ⓑ Ⓒ Ⓓ	94 Ⓐ Ⓑ Ⓒ Ⓓ
20 Ⓐ Ⓑ Ⓒ Ⓓ	45 Ⓐ Ⓑ Ⓒ Ⓓ	70 Ⓐ Ⓑ Ⓒ Ⓓ	95 Ⓐ Ⓑ Ⓒ Ⓓ
21 Ⓐ Ⓑ Ⓒ Ⓓ	46 Ⓐ Ⓑ Ⓒ Ⓓ	71 Ⓐ Ⓑ Ⓒ Ⓓ	96 Ⓐ Ⓑ Ⓒ Ⓓ
22 Ⓐ Ⓑ Ⓒ Ⓓ	47 Ⓐ Ⓑ Ⓒ Ⓓ	72 Ⓐ Ⓑ Ⓒ Ⓓ	97 Ⓐ Ⓑ Ⓒ Ⓓ
23 Ⓐ Ⓑ Ⓒ Ⓓ	48 Ⓐ Ⓑ Ⓒ Ⓓ	73 Ⓐ Ⓑ Ⓒ Ⓓ	98 Ⓐ Ⓑ Ⓒ Ⓓ
24 Ⓐ Ⓑ Ⓒ Ⓓ	49 Ⓐ Ⓑ Ⓒ Ⓓ	74 Ⓐ Ⓑ Ⓒ Ⓓ	99 Ⓐ Ⓑ Ⓒ Ⓓ
25 Ⓐ Ⓑ Ⓒ Ⓓ	50 Ⓐ Ⓑ Ⓒ Ⓓ	75 Ⓐ Ⓑ Ⓒ Ⓓ	100 Ⓐ Ⓑ Ⓒ Ⓓ

MILLER ANALOGIES SAMPLE TEST V

1. FEAST : MEAL :: VELLUM : (a. paper, b. fur, c. cotton, d. forest)

2. (a. leave, b. audition, c. divide, d. correct) : APPLY :: PART : POSITION

3. OXEN : STRENGTH :: (a. furnace, b. animal, c. cattle, d. ants) : INDUSTRY

4. ASSIDUOUS : EGREGIOUS :: (a. leafy, b. desultory, c. diligent, d. bitter) : FLAGRANT

5. SHIP : (a. crow's nest, b. deck, c. prow, d. mast) :: COLUMN : CAPITAL

6. DAVID COPPERFIELD : TINY TIM :: (a. Joseph Andrews, b. Ahab, c. Becky Sharp, d. Little Nell) : OLIVER TWIST

7. CLEOPATRA : (a. Caesar, b. poison, c. Anthony, d. beauty) :: GOLIATH : STONE

8. (a. circle, b. heart, c. dissemination, d. artery) : CIRCULATE :: DITCH : IRRIGATE

9. BRIGHT : GAUDY :: (a. urged, b. driven, c. prevented, d. acquiesced) : COMPELLED

10. (a. dissidence, b. deficiency, c. irreverence, d. deference) : DISRE-SPECT :: IMBUE : EXTRACT

11. EGO : ID :: SELF : (a. desire, b. society, c. conscience, d. morality)

12. HIGH GEAR : (a. automobile, b. driver, c. speed, d. brake) :: PROGRESS : RECESSION

13. (a. gem, b. spore, c. illegitimacy, d. superficiality) : SPURIOUS :: MONEY : COUNTERFEIT

14. BRINE : LANE :: PINE : (a. oak, b. line, c. stain, d. dross)

15. 135 : 9 :: 251 : (a. 8, b. 12, c. 7, d. 10)

16. QUEUE : (a. borough, b. tail, c. line, d. broom) :: CUE : BROUGHAM

17. COLONEL : REGIMENT :: (a. major, b. captain, c. private, d. general) : BATTALION

18. DILETTANTE : (a. thorough, b. painstaking, c. diplomatic, d. superficial) :: HOYDEN : CAREFREE

19. RECEIVER : DIAL :: SPEAKERS : (a. talk, b. stylus, c. tray, d. template)

20. (a. rectify, b. make, c. find, d. realize) : MISTAKE :: REGAIN : LOSS

21. INDEX : FRONTISPIECE :: MATURITY : (a. adolescence, b. infancy, c. puberty, d. adulthood)

22. TAUTOLOGICAL : REDUNDANT :: (a. mature, b. incipient, c. concealed, d. late) : INCHOATE

23. SQUARE : (a. triangle, b. triplet, c. poem, d. duet) :: QUADRUPLET : COUPLET

24. HOPE : (a. horn, b. charity, c. tempest, d. despair) :: FEAR : COD

25. (a. m, b. p, c. l, d. t) : H :: W : S

26. CHOLERIC : PHLEGMATIC :: (a. timid, b. blind, c. mute, d. temerarious) : CIRCUMSPECT

27. IRON : (a. hard, b. strong, c. steel, d. pig) :: OIL : CRUDE

28. (a. astronomy, b. play, c. symphony, d. heavens) : STAR :: CONCERT : SOLOIST

29. SALUTE : (a. motto, b. reveille, c. mess, d. orders) :: TROOP : EAGLE

30. PROVISIONS : QUARTERMASTER :: (a. cup, b. knife, c. saddle, d. manuscript) : SCRIVENER

31. ATLANTIS : (a. Pompeii, b. Xanadu, c. Byzantium, d. Zanzibar) :: SHANGRI-LA : EL DORADO

32. WIND : DEFICIT :: EROSION : (a. spending, b. appreciation, c. borrowing, d. employment)

33. (a. slot, b. note, c. band, d. harmony) : VALVE :: HARMONICA : TRUMPET

34. FLAUNT : (a. destructively, b. stupidly, c. willingly, d. boastfully) :: BETRAY : DECEPTIVELY

35. HOUYHNHNM : YAHOO :: REASON : (a. learning, b. intelligence, c. ignorance, d. genius)

36. DEFIED : ASTRIDE :: EARTH : (a. geography, b. zoology, c. birth, d. life)

37. ISTANBUL : CONSTANTINOPLE :: (a. Stalingrad, b. Leningrad, c. Moscow, d. Odessa) : ST. PETERSBURG

38. (a. 1899, b. 1900, c. 1901, d. 1902) : 1910 :: 1950 : 1959

39. ADVOCATE : (a. impute, b. allude, c. imply, d. impugn) :: AMELIO-RATE : IMPAIR

40. HENRY MOORE : (a. Rodin, b. Pavlov, c. Van Gogh, d. Gertrude Stein) :: DONATELLO : BERNINI

41. PLANE : CYCLE :: (a. air, b. angle, c. foot, d. led) : COLOR

42. HEDGER : SHRUBBERY :: (a. snuffer, b. cougher, c. whittler, d. stickler) : STICK

43. MAN : (a. bird, b. centipede, c. elephant, d. Adam) :: WHEELBARROW : BICYCLE

44. (a. velocity, b. viscosity, c. temperature, d. density) : FLUID :: FRIC-TION : SOLID

45. CANTON : COUNTRY :: (a. Ohio, b. Japan, c. Switzerland, d. China) : IRELAND

46. PECK : PINT :: 1 : (a. 4, b. 16, c. 8, d. 2)

47. TWEEZERS : BLEACH :: (a. steel, b. light, c. adding machine, d. eraser) : PICKPOCKET

48. JAWBONING : (a. persuade, b. filet, c. cleaning, d. arbitrate) :: FILIBUSTERING : OBSTRUCT

49. SHERRY : BEER :: PORT : (a. champagne, b. sauterne, c. claret, d. muscatel)

50. HONOR : GOVERNOR :: (a. Excellency, b. Majesty, c. Highness, d. Grace) : DUKE

51. ANDIRON : PEDESTAL :: (a. log, b. bucket, c. anvil, d. skillet) : STATUE

52. GENERAL : STARS :: COLONEL : (a. oak, b. silver, c. gold, d. eagle)

53. (a. insist, b. reply, c. demur, d. demand) : REFUSE :: LAZY : INERT

54. HEART : HEAD :: VENERY : (a. ribaldry, b. flesh, c. mortality, d. restraint)

55. CALORIE : (a. energy, b. weight, c. metabolism, d. food) :: CENTURY : TIME

56. FLORIDA : SAUDI ARABIA :: (a. Louisiana, b. Georgia, c. Arkansas, d. Iraq) : IRAN

57. GNAT : (a. kimono, b. spagetti, c. embarrassment, d. perseverance) :: ACCOMMODATION : ECSTACY

58. BOARDWALK : (a. Park Place, b. Atlantic City, c. display, d. escalator) :: STRAND : STORE

59. (a. Parliament, b. Congress, c. Great Britain, d. Senate) : LORDS :: HOUSE : COMMONS

60. IBLE : ABLE :: TON : (a. acy, b. cry, c. wich, d. itis)

61. MALLARD : CANVASBACK :: (a. knee, b. Scottish, c. drake, d. gander) : ARGYLE

62. SERIOUS : (a. laconic, b. garrulous, c. deaf, d. puzzled) :: HUNGRY : IMPECUNIOUS

63. LAERTES : (a. Odysseus, b. Polonius, c. Claudius, d. Ophelia) :: ICARUS : DAEDALUS

64. SYRACUSE : (a. Oneonta, b. Geneva, c. Raleigh, d. Goshen) :: CARTHAGE : ALEXANDRIA

65. PALL : CLOY :: (a. obbligato, b. innuendo, c. declaration, d. crescendo) : INSINUATION

66. ORGANISM : (a. plant, b. animal, c. bacteria, d. cell) :: LIGHT : WAVE

67. KOLN : WEIN :: COLOGNE : (a. Vienna, b. Prague, c. Warsaw, d. Hamburg)

68. SEDIMENT : DIME :: (a. discussion, b. debate, c. argument, d. rally) : GUM

69. WISDOM : (a. lion, b. owl, c. fox, d. deer) :: SPRING : ROBIN

70. BUTTERFLY : (a. insect, b. silkworm, c. wings, d. summer) :: CHRYSA-LIS : COCOON

71. ICELAND : NORWAY :: (a. winter, b. queen, c. president, d. sovereign) : KING

72. (a. discourse, b. plot, c. Olympics, d. Greek) : PLATO :: TEAM : MANET

73. CYLINDER : LOCK :: MOTOR : (a. shaft, b. canal, c. tackle, d. escape)

74. BANANA : (a. sapphire, b. saltcellar, c. stone, d. tree) :: BUTTER : SKY

75. GNASH : TEETH :: (a. fold, b. clasp, c. gnarl, d. wring) : HANDS

76. (a. opossum, b. fox, c. beaver, d. lady) : KANGAROO :: CHICKEN : COCKROACH

77. APHRODITE : VENUS :: ARES : (a. Mercury, b. Mars, c. Apollo, d. Hermes)

78. (a. toast, b. under, c. show, d. coffee) : DAY :: TEA : OVER

79. CLARINET : PIANO :: WIND : (a. reed, b. wood, c. percussion, d. pianist)

80. ELEVATOR : SKYSCRAPER :: (a. escalator, b. companionway, c. bulkhead, d. bridge) : SHIP

81. PROPENSITY : (a. riches, b. weight, c. bias, d. thought) :: CLUB : MACE

82. SALZBURG : STRATFORD :: (a. Goethe, b. Avon, c. Mozart, d. Brahms) SHAKESPEARE

83. FLAMMABLE : INFLAMMABLE :: PERTINENT : (a. impertinent, b. inopportune, c. incoherent, d. relevant)

84. (a. revolution, b. dance, c. torque, d. axis) : ROTATE :: FRICTION : RESIST

85. PRISM : (a. spectrum, b. reflection, c. light, d. binoculars) :: FAMINE : WANT

86. LOOP : HUB :: BEEF : (a. corn, b. beans, c. tobacco, d. cotton)

87. JANUARY : (a. Cleveland, b. June, c. Washington, d. Hermes) :: SUNDAY : MERCURY

88. LIFT : ELEVATOR :: (a. oil, b. grease, c. gas, d. petrol) : GASOLINE

89. (a. 1/6, b. 4/5, c. 2/5, d. 2/10) : 1/10 :: 3/4 : 3/16

90. TORT : LITIGATION :: CONTRACT : (a. signature, b. obligation, c. clause, d. equity)

91. BULL : (a. wolf, b. turtle, c. fish, d. snail) :: CRAB : LION

92. EQUINOX : SOLSTICE :: SEPTEMBER : (a. November, b. January, c. June, d. March)

93. (a. hand, b. brow, c. rose, d. soon) : KNIT :: DICTATION : TAKE

94. GARROTING : DEATH :: CANVASSING : (a. painting, b. shelter, c. votes, d. fight)

95. (a. philosophy, b. wreath, c. mountain, d. restaurant) : INSINCERITY :: SLAVERY : LOVE

96. SICKLE : RUSSIA :: (a. scythe, b. crescent, c. Caspian, d. hammer) : TURKEY

97. CICERO : DEMOSTHENES :: ROOSEVELT : (a. MacArthur, b. Hemingway, c. Shaw, d. Churchill)

98. TYRO : (a. tyrant, b. master, c. amateur, d. dabbler) :: TURPITUDE : PROBITY

99. COKE : COAL :: (a. firewood, b. planks, c. saw, d. lumberjack) : TIMBER

100. SHOE: (a. fly, b. cobbler, c. pair, d. bell) :: SAW : GEAR

ANSWER KEY FOR MILLER ANALOGIES SAMPLE TEST V

1.	a	21.	b	41.	b	61.	a	81.	c
2.	b	22.	b	42.	c	62.	a	82.	c
3.	d	23.	d	43.	c	63.	b	83.	d
4.	c	24.	a	44.	b	64.	d	84.	c
5.	a	25.	c	45.	c	65.	b	85.	a
6.	d	26.	d	46.	b	66.	d	86.	b
7.	b	27.	d	47.	d	67.	a	87.	c
8.	d	28.	b	48.	a	68.	c	88.	d
9.	a	29.	a	49.	a	69.	b	89.	c
10.	d	30.	d	50.	d	70.	b	90.	b
11.	a	31.	b	51.	a	71.	c	91.	c
12.	d	32.	c	52.	d	72.	b	92.	c
13.	a	33.	a	53.	c	73.	b	93.	b
14.	c	34.	d	54.	d	74.	a	94.	c
15.	a	35.	c	55.	a	75.	d	95.	a
16.	d	36.	c	56.	a	76.	a	96.	b
17.	a	37.	b	57.	b	77.	b	97.	d
18.	d	38.	c	58.	d	78.	c	98.	b
19.	b	39.	d	59.	d	79.	c	99.	b
20.	a	40.	a	60.	c	80.	b	100.	d

EXPLANATORY ANSWERS FOR
MILLER ANALOGIES SAMPLE TEST V

1. (a) In this analogy of degree, a FEAST is a rich and expensive MEAL; VELLUM is a rich and expensive kind of PAPER.

2. (b) The correspondence is one of action to object. You APPLY for a POSITION of employment; you AUDITION for a PART in a play.

3. (d) In this association analogy, OXEN are associated with STRENGTH; ANTS are associated with INDUSTRY.

4. (c) In this synonym analogy, another word for EGREGIOUS is FLAGRANT and a synonym for ASSIDUOUS is DILIGENT.

5. (a) A CROW'S NEST is a small observation platform near the top of the mast of a SHIP; a CAPITAL is the uppermost part of a COLUMN.

6. (d) The relationship among DAVID COPPERFIELD, TINY TIM and OLIVER TWIST is that they are all fictional characters created by Charles Dickens. To complete the analogy, another Dickens character must be selected, and LITTLE NELL is the correct choice.

7. (b) GOLIATH was killed by a STONE; CLEOPATRA was killed by POISON.

8. (d) In this object-to-action analogy, a DITCH is the channel through which water flows to IRRIGATE; an ARTERY is the vessel or channel through which blood may CIRCULATE.

9. (a) The relationship is one of degree since GAUDY is excessively BRIGHT; COMPELLED is excessively URGED.

10. (d) IMBUE, meaning to permeate, is the opposite of EXTRACT, meaning to draw out. The opposite of DISRESPECT is DEFERENCE.

11. (a) EGO is a psychological term for SELF; ID is a psychological term for DESIRE.

12. (d) A HIGH GEAR and a BRAKE have opposite functions; similarly, PROGRESS and RECESSION are opposite in meaning.

13. (a) A GEM is worthless when it is SPURIOUS; MONEY is worthless when it is COUNTERFEIT.

14. (c) This is a non-semantic rhyming analogy. BRINE rhymes with PINE and LANE rhymes with STAIN.

15. (a) In the number 135, the digits add up to 9 (1 + 3 + 5 = 9). Similarly, in the number 251, the digits add up to 8 (2 + 5 + 1 = 8).

16. (d) QUEUE and CUE are homophones, different in meaning but pronounced the same; BROOM and BROUGHAM are also pronounced the same.

17. (a) A COLONEL leads a REGIMENT; a MAJOR leads a BATTALION.

18. (d) This is a characteristic analogy. A characteristic of a HOYDEN is her CAREFREE attitude; a characteristic of a DILETTANTE, a dabbler, is a tendency to be SUPERFICIAL.

19. (b) This a part-to-part analogy. A RECEIVER and a DIAL are parts of a telephone; SPEAKERS and a STYLUS, the needle, are parts of a record player.

20. (a) The relationship is one of action to object. To improve a poor or unfortunate condition one may RECTIFY a MISTAKE, and one may REGAIN a LOSS.

21. (b) In this sequence analogy, the INDEX comes at the end of a book, the FRONTISPIECE comes at the beginning; MATURITY comes in the latter part of life, INFANCY comes at the beginning.

22. (b) TAUTOLOGICAL is a synonym for REDUNDANT; INCHOATE, which means at an early stage of development, is a synonym for INCIPIENT.

23. (d) A QUADRUPLET is any group of four; a COUPLET consists of two successive rhyming lines of verse. Because a SQUARE has four sides, to complete the analogy a term must be chosen that involves a pair, and DUET, a composition for two performers, is the only possible choice.

24. (a) In this place analogy, HOPE, FEAR and COD are all names of capes. To complete the analogy another cape must be selected and Cape HORN is the correct choice.

25. (c) In the alphabet, L is the fourth letter after H; W is the fourth letter after S.

26. (d) CHOLERIC, which means bad-tempered, and PHLEGMATIC, meaning easy-going, are opposites; TEMERARIOUS, which means rash and reckless, and CIRCUMSPECT, meaning careful, are opposites.

27. (d) In this product-to-source analogy, OIL in its rough state is called CRUDE oil; IRON in its rough state is called PIG iron.

28. (b) A STAR takes the leading role in a PLAY; a SOLOIST takes the leading role in a CONCERT.

29. (a) A SALUTE, TROOP and EAGLE are all things associated with the boy scouts. To complete the analogy another element of scouting should be selected, and MOTTO is the correct choice.

30. (d) In this worker-to-job analogy, a QUARTERMASTER's job is to secure PROVISIONS for an army; a SCRIVENER's job is to copy a MANUSCRIPT.

31. (b) ATLANTIS, SHANGRI-LA and EL DORADO are related because each is a mythical place. XANADU, the only mythical place among the answer choices, correctly completes this analogy.

32. (c) In this cause-and-effect analogy, one effect of excessive WIND is soil EROSION; an effect of an excessive DEFICIT is BORROWING to make up for expenditures. Excessive spending is a cause of a deficit, not an effect.

33. (a) The correspondence is one of part to whole. A VALVE is part of a TRUMPET; a SLOT is part of a HARMONICA.

34. (d) To FLAUNT is to act BOASTFULLY; to BETRAY is to act DECEPTIVELY.

35. (c) In *Gulliver's Travels* by Jonathan Swift, a HOUYHNHNM symbolizes intelligence and REASON, whereas a YAHOO symbolizes the opposite, stupidity or IGNORANCE.

36. (c) In this non-semantic rhyming analogy, DEFIED rhymes with ASTRIDE; EARTH rhymes with BIRTH.

37. (b) ISTANBUL was formerly called CONSTANTINOPLE; LENINGRAD was formerly called ST. PETERSBURG.

38. (c) In this sequence analogy, the difference between 1901 and 1910 is nine years; the difference between 1950 and 1959 is nine years.

39. (d) AMELIORATE, meaning to improve or to make better, is the opposite of IMPAIR, meaning to make worse. The opposite of ADVOCATE, meaning to support or to plead in favor of, is IMPUGN, meaning to deny or to attack as false.

40. (a) The connection among HENRY MOORE, DONATELLO, and BERNINI is that they are all sculptors. To complete the analogy, another sculptor must be chosen, and RODIN is the correct choice.

41. (b) This is a prefix analogy. PLANE and CYCLE are related because they commonly appear with the prefix *bi* (biplane and bicycle). COLOR may take the prefix *tri* (tricolor). The only other word that may also take a *tri* prefix is ANGLE (triangle).

42. (c) A HEDGER trims SHRUBBERY; a WHITTLER trims a STICK.

43. (c) The relationship is a numerical ratio of one to two. A WHEELBARROW has one wheel; a BICYCLE has two. Similarly, a MAN has two legs, and an ELEPHANT has four.

44. (b) VISCOSITY is the resistance of a FLUID to flow just as FRICTION is the resistance to relative motion between two SOLIDs.

45. (c) A CANTON is a territorial division in SWITZERLAND; a COUNTY is a territorial division in IRELAND.

46. (b) In this measurement analogy, a PECK is equal to 8 quarts. A PINT is half of a quart; therefore, 1 peck is equal to 16 pints.

47. (c) The relationship among TWEEZERS, BLEACH and a PICKPOCKET is that they all remove something. Among the choices, an ERASER also removes something, a mistake.

48. (a) In this purpose analogy, a purpose of FILIBUSTERING is to OBSTRUCT passage of legislation. The purpose of JAWBONING is to PERSUADE or coax another party to accept your position.

49. (a) SHERRY has no carbonation; BEER has carbonation; PORT has no carbonation; CHAMPAGNE has carbonation.

50. (d) The proper way to refer to people in certain positions or ranks is to say his HONOR, the GOVERNOR, and his GRACE, the DUKE.

51. (a) An ANDIRON holds a LOG; a PEDESTAL holds a STATUE.

52. (d) In this association analogy, STARS symbolize the rank of GEN-ERAL; an EAGLE symbolizes the rank of COLONEL.

53. (c) The relationship is one of degree. LAZY is a lesser degree of mobility than INERT; DEMUR is a lesser degree of protestation than REFUSE.

54. (d) It is often said that the ways of the HEART are the opposite to the ways of the HEAD; the opposite of VENERY, the gratification of desires, is RESTRAINT.

55. (a) A CALORIE is a measure of the heat-producing or ENERGY-producing value of food. A CENTURY is a measure of TIME.

56. (a) In this place analogy, SAUDI ARABIA and IRAN are both countries bordering on the Persian Gulf; FLORIDA and LOUISIANA are states which border on the Gulf of Mexico.

57. (b) ACCOMMODATION is spelled correctly, but ECSTACY is spelled incorrectly (it should be *ecstasy*); GNAT is spelled correctly, and SPAGETTI is spelled incorrectly (it should be *spaghetti*).

58. (d) A BOARDWALK is a kind of walkway along a STRAND or beach; an ESCALATOR is a kind of walkway in a department STORE.

59. (d) The SENATE and the House of LORDS are the two upper houses of the U.S. Congress and the British Parliament respectively; the HOUSE of Representatives and House of COMMONS are the two lower houses.

60. (c) IBLE and ABLE are suffixes meaning able; TON and WICH are suffixes referring to towns.

61. (a) In this classification analogy, the relationship between a MALLARD and a CANVASBACK is that they are both kinds of ducks. The relationship between ARGYLE and KNEE is that they are both kinds of socks.

62. (a) Since an IMPECUNIOUS person is usually penniless, he is likely to be HUNGRY; since a LACONIC person is one of few words, he is likely to be SERIOUS.

63. (b) In Greek mythology, ICARUS is the son of DAEDALUS; in Shakespeare's play *Hamlet*, LAERTES is the son of POLONIUS.

64. (d) SYRACUSE, GOSHEN, CARTHAGE and ALEXANDRIA are all names of ancient historical communities.

65. (b) PALL and CLOY are synonyms; INNUENDO and INSINUATION are also synonyms.

66. (d) In this whole-to-part analogy, an ORGANISM is made up of CELLs; LIGHT consists physically of WAVEs.

67. (a) The German name for COLOGNE is KÖLN; the German name for VIENNA is WIEN.

68. (c) In this non-semantic word-within-a-word analogy, DIME is part of the word SEDIMENT; GUM is part of the word ARGUMENT.

69. (b) The relationship is one of association. A ROBIN is associated with the coming of SPRING; an OWL is associated with great WISDOM.

70. (b) An early stage in the development of the BUTTERFLY is the CHRYSALIS; an early stage in the development of the SILKWORM is the COCOON.

71. (c) ICELAND is a republic headed by a PRESIDENT; NORWAY is a monarchy headed by a KING.

72. (b) The name PLATO includes the four letters of the word PLOT; the name MANET includes the four letters of the word TEAM.

73. (b) A CYLINDER is part of a MOTOR; a LOCK is part of a CANAL.

74. (a) BUTTER is yellow and SKY is blue; since a BANANA is yellow, the task is to find the choice that is blue, a SAPPHIRE.

75. (d) In this action-to-object analogy, you may GNASH your TEETH or WRING your HANDS in anger or dismay. All of the other choices are also activities that can be done with your hands but they are not characteristically a sign of anger or dismay.

76. (a) An OPOSSUM and a KANGAROO are both classified as marsupial; a CHICKEN and COCKROACH are both related as oviparous.

77. (b) APHRODITE is the Greek goddess of love and beauty; VENUS is her Roman counterpart. ARES is the Greek god of war and MARS is the Roman counterpart.

78. (c) DAY, TEA and OVER are all words associated with time (daytime, tea time and overtime). To complete the analogy, another word associated with time must be selected, and SHOW (show time) is the correct choice.

79. (c) A CLARINET is a WIND instrument; a PIANO is a PERCUSSION instrument.

80. (b) An ELEVATOR is used to ascend and descend in a SKYSCRAPER; a COMPANIONWAY is used for the same purpose in a SHIP.

81. (c) In this degree analogy, a PROPENSITY is a lesser degree of opinion than is a BIAS; a CLUB is a less ominous weapon than a MACE.

82. (c) STRATFORD is the birthplace of SHAKESPEARE; SALZBURG is the birthplace of MOZART.

83. (d) FLAMMABLE and INFLAMMABLE are synonyms; PERTINENT and RELEVANT are also synonyms.

84. (c) In this cause-and-effect analogy, FRICTION causes something to RESIST moving; TORQUE causes something to ROTATE.

85. (a) In this product-source analogy, a SPECTRUM is created by a PRISM; WANT is produced by a FAMINE.

86. (b) The LOOP and the HUB are nicknames for Chicago and Boston respectively; Chicago is known for its BEEF, and Boston is known for its BEANS.

87. (c) We have a number of firsts here: JANUARY is the first month; SUNDAY is the first day of the week; MERCURY is the first planet in distance from the sun; and WASHINGTON was the first U.S. president.

88. (d) LIFT is the British word for an ELEVATOR; PETROL is the British word for GASOLINE.

89. (c) In this numerical analogy, 1/4 of 3/4 is 3/16; 1/4 of 2/5 is 1/10.

90. (b) A TORT is a wrong that entails LITIGATION; a CONTRACT is an agreement that entails OBLIGATION.

91. (c) The BULL (Taurus), FISH (Pisces), CRAB (Cancer), and LION (Leo) are all signs of the zodiac.

92. (c) EQUINOX refers to either of the two times each year when the sun crosses the equator and day and night are everywhere of equal length, occurring about March 21 and SEPTEMBER 23. SOLSTICE refers to

one of the two points at which the sun's apparent position on the celestial sphere reaches its greatest distance above or below the celestial equator, occurring about JUNE 22 and December 22.

93. (b) In this action-to-object analogy, one may KNIT a BROW and one may TAKE DICTATION.

94. (c) The correspondence is one of cause and effect. GARROTING (strangling) commonly causes DEATH; CANVASSING (soliciting for support) commonly results in VOTES.

95. (a) INSINCERITY, SLAVERY and LOVE are all related because they are abstract nouns. PHILOSOPHY is also an abstract noun.

96. (b) In this symbol analogy, the SICKLE (in conjunction with the hammer) is a symbol of RUSSIA; the CRESCENT is a symbol of TURKEY.

97. (d) CICERO and DEMOSTHENES are related as orators; ROOSE-VELT and CHURCHILL are related as statesmen.

98. (b) The opposite of TURPITUDE, which means baseness, is PROBITY, meaning uprightness. An antonym for TYRO, a beginner, is MASTER.

99. (b) In this product-source analogy, COKE is obtained by heating COAL; PLANKS are formed by cutting TIMBER.

100. (d) A SAW and a GEAR both have teeth; a SHOE and a BELL both have a tongue.

Part Three
Verbal Analogies for College Entrance and Other Graduate-level Examinations

ANALOGY PAIRS

Because the analogy question provides a measure of both vocabulary and reasoning ability, it is an important component of many tests of general intelligence and verbal ability. Such well-known examinations as the Scholastic Aptitude Test (SAT), the Graduate Record Examination (GRE) and the Graduate Management Admission Test (GMAT) all include verbal analogy questions.

These tests, however, present the analogy problem in a slightly different form. Instead of supplying only one missing term as on the MAT, you must select a pair of words whose relationship to each other most closely parallels the relationship expressed by the first word pair.

Sample Analogy Pair
SNAPSHOT : SCRAPBOOK ::
(A) memo : file
(B) photograph : book jacket
(C) camera : case
(D) film : frame
(E) career : portfolio

Answer: (A) A SNAPSHOT is stored for future reference in a SCRAPBOOK in the same way that a MEMO is stored in a FILE.

Although the format of these analogy problems differs from the format of MAT problems, the same strategies apply. First you must determine the nature of the relationship between the terms of the given word pair, and then you must select the one pair from the choices offered in which the terms are related in exactly the same way.

You'll get plenty of practice with this type of analogy problem in the pages that follow. The practice questions are divided into short tests in order to allow you to complete a set even when you have only a few minutes to spare. After each test you will find both correct and explanatory answers for each question.

TEST I. ANALOGY PAIRS
TIME: 10 Minutes. 20 Questions.

Directions: Each of these test questions begins with two CAPITAL-IZED words which are related to each other in some way. Find out how they are related. Then study the five pairs of words that follow. They are lettered (A) (B) (C) (D) (E). Select the two words which are related to each other in the same way that the two CAPITALIZED words are related.

1. LINEAR : CURVILINEAR ::
   (A) throw: reach
   (B) sunrise : sunset
   (C) absolute : relative
   (D) arrow : bow
   (E) bow : arrow

2. LETTUCE : LEAF ::
   (A) potato : eye
   (B) rose : thorn
   (C) onion : bulb
   (D) grass : stem
   (E) grape : vine

3. SODIUM : SALT ::
   (A) soda : solution
   (B) molecule : atom
   (C) oxygen : water
   (D) chemistry : biochemistry
   (E) analysis : synthesis

4. DAM : WATER ::
   (A) over : under
   (B) embargo : trade
   (C) curse : H$_2$O
   (D) beaver : fish
   (E) river : stream

5. ALLAY : PAIN ::
   (A) damp : noise
   (B) create : noise
   (C) regain : consciousness
   (D) fray : edge
   (E) soothe : nerves

6. LATENT : LATE ::
   (A) crude : callous
   (B) potential : tardy

(C) natty : nettled
(D) obvious : concealed
(E) decorous : deceased

7. CALIBER : RIFLE ::
   (A) reputation : blast
   (B) compass : bore
   (C) army : navy
   (D) gauge : rails
   (E) cavalry : infantry

8. CHOP : MINCE ::
   (A) fry : bake
   (B) meat : cake
   (C) axe : mallet
   (D) Washington : Lincoln
   (E) stir : beat

9. PECCADILLO : CRIME ::
   (A) district attorney : criminal
   (B) hesitate : procrastinate
   (C) armadillo : bone
   (D) bushel : peck
   (E) sheriff : jail

10. WOOD : PAPER ::
    (A) iron : steel
    (B) chair : wall
    (C) cut : clip
    (D) fireplace : lighter
    (E) forest : fire

11. FRENETIC : SANGUINE ::
    (A) cool : hot
    (B) ardent : involved
    (C) frantic : unruffled
    (D) unharried : unsullied
    (E) uncouth : rude

12. COMPETITION : COMPEN-
 SATION ::
   (A) absurdity : serenity
   (B) commendation : condensa-
    tion
   (C) contending : amends
   (D) striving : contriving
   (E) geniality : cordiality

13. CANDID : DEVIOUS ::
   (A) unnerved : unhinged
   (B) unruffled : unnerved
   (C) unhinged : unspoken
   (D) unsullied : unruffled
   (E) upright : underhanded

14. PUBLICATION : LIBEL ::
   (A) newspaper : editorial
   (B) radio : television
   (C) information : liability
   (D) journalism : attack
   (E) speech : slander

15. CANAL : PANAMA ::
   (A) sea : land
   (B) ships : commerce
   (C) chord : circle
   (D) locks : waterway
   (E) country : continent

16. ALLEVIATE : AGGRA-
 VATE ::
   (A) joke : worry

   (B) elevate : agree
   (C) level : grade
   (D) plastic : rigid
   (E) alluvial : gravelly

17. BEHAVIOR : IMPRO-
 PRIETY ::
   (A) honesty : morality
   (B) freedom : servitude
   (C) response : stimulus
   (D) word : malapropism
   (E) grammar : usage

18. ELM : TREE ::
   (A) dollar : dime
   (B) currency : dime
   (C) map : leaves
   (D) oak : maple
   (E) dollar : money

19. DOCTOR : DISEASE ::
   (A) miser : money
   (B) illness : prescription
   (C) sheriff : crime
   (D) theft : punishment
   (E) intern : hospital

20. EXAMINATION : CHEAT ::
   (A) lawyer : defendant
   (B) compromise : principles
   (C) army : gripe
   (D) swindle : business
   (E) politics : graft

CORRECT ANSWERS

1. D	4. B	7. D	10. A	13. E	16. D	19. C
2. C	5. A	8. E	11. C	14. E	17. D	20. E
3. C	6. B	9. B	12. C	15. C	18. E	

EXPLANATORY ANSWERS TEST I. ANALOGY PAIRS

1. (D) LINEAR and CURVILIN-EAR refer to equations which, when graphed, describe straight and curved lines respectively. The only answer choice that suggests first a straight and then a curved line is ARROW : BOW. Choice (E) is incorrect because the order of the shapes is reversed.

2. (C) Humans consider both the LEAF of the LETTUCE and the BULB of the ONION to be edible.

3. (C) SODIUM is one of the elements that make up SALT; OXYGEN is one of the elements that make up WATER.

4. (B) A DAM obstructs the flow of WATER; an EMBARGO obstructs the flow of TRADE.

5. (A) One ALLAYS (reduces) PAIN; one DAMPS (reduces) NOISE.

6. (B) LATENT means POTENTIAL; LATE means TARDY.

7. (D) CALIBER is a standard of measurement for a RIFLE; GAUGE is a standard of measurement for RAILS.

8. (E) To MINCE is more extreme than to CHOP; to BEAT is more extreme than to STIR.

9. (B) A PECCADILLO is a small offense; a CRIME is a large one. To HESITATE is brief; to PROCRASTINATE is extended.

10. (A) WOOD is used to make PAPER; IRON is used to make STEEL.

11. (C) FRENETIC and SANGUINE are opposites meaning the same as FRANTIC and UNRUFFLED respectively. Choice (A) is incorrect because the opposites are in reverse order.

12. (C) Since there appears to be no functional relationship between COMPETITION and COMPENSATION, look for an answer which provides a synonym for each word. Only (C) CONTENDING : AMENDS provides synonyms for both key words.

13. (E) CANDID and DEVIOUS are antonyms. Both (B) and (E) provide antonym pairs; however, (E) is the better match for the key pair because UPRIGHT means the same as candid and UNDERHANDED means the same as devious.

14. (E) LIBEL is written defamation; it appears in a PUBLICATION. SLANDER is oral defamation; it appears in SPEECH.

15. (C) A CANAL cuts right through the country of PANAMA; a CHORD cuts right through a CIRCLE.

16. (D) ALLEVIATE and AGGRAVATE are antonyms, so are PLASTIC and RIGID.

17. (D) An unacceptable form of

BEHAVIOR is an IMPROPRI-ETY; an incorrect use of a WORD is a MALAPROPISM.

18. (E) An ELM is a type of TREE; a DOLLAR is a type of MONEY.

19. (C) A DOCTOR seeks to elimi-nate DISEASE; a SHERIFF seeks to eliminate CRIME.

20. (E) To CHEAT on an EXAMI-NATION is against regulations; to accept GRAFT in POLI-TICS is against the law.

TEST II. ANALOGY PAIRS
TIME : 10 Minutes. 20 Questions.

Directions: Each of these test questions begins with two CAPITAL-IZED words which are related to each other in some way. Find out how they are related. Then study the five pairs of words that follow. They are lettered (A)(B)(C)(D)(E). Select the two words which are related to each other in the same way that the two CAPITALIZED words are related.

1. ADVERSITY : HAPPINESS ::
   (A) fear : misfortune
   (B) solace : adversity
   (C) vehemence : serenity
   (D) troublesome : petulance
   (E) graduation : felicitation

2. LUTE : STRING ::
   (A) flute : treble
   (B) xylophone : percussion
   (C) drum : rhythm
   (D) violin : concert
   (E) piano : octave

3. FEATHERS : PLUCK ::
   (A) goose : duck
   (B) garment : weave
   (C) car : drive
   (D) wool : shear
   (E) duck : down

4. MODESTY : ARROGANCE ::
   (A) debility : strength
   (B) cause : purpose
   (C) passion : emotion
   (D) finance : Wall Street
   (E) practice : perfection

5. BLOW : HORN ::
   (A) switch : tracks
   (B) tune : lights
   (C) go over : map
   (D) accelerate : engine
   (E) turn on : radio

6. BAY : SEA ::
   (A) mountain : valley
   (B) plain : forest
   (C) peninsula : land
   (D) cape : reef
   (E) island : sound

7. DECEMBER : WINTER ::
   (A) April : showers
   (B) September : summer
   (C) June : fall
   (D) March : spring
   (E) February : autumn

8. PRODIGAL : SPEND-THRIFT ::
   (A) rash : brave
   (B) foolhardy : foolish
   (C) near-sighted : myopic
   (D) dangerous : lethal
   (E) profligate : lavish

9. AERIALIST : MINER ::
   (A) subterranean : aetherial
   (B) flier : youth
   (C) terrestrial : celestial
   (D) trapeze : pick
   (E) arboreal : sartorial

10. INTERRUPT : SPEAK ::
    (A) shout : yell
    (B) intrude : enter
    (C) assist : interfere
    (D) telephone : telegraph
    (E) concede : defend

11. ENCOURAGE : RESTRICT::
    (A) gain : succeed
    (B) deprive : supply
    (C) see : believe
    (D) detain : deny
    (E) finish : complete

12. BEFOUL : TIDY ::
    (A) animate : inanimate
    (B) extricate : intricate
    (C) introvert : extrovert
    (D) cloth : clergy
    (E) indict : acquit

13. ITALY : MILAN ::
    (A) Paris : Moscow
    (B) Moscow : Russia
    (C) Spain : Madrid
    (D) Manhattan : New York
    (E) Norway : Sweden

14. MIST : RAIN ::
    (A) wind : hurricane
    (B) hail : thunder
    (C) snow : freeze
    (D) clouds : sky
    (E) sun : warm

15. GUN : HOLSTER ::
    (A) shoe : soldier
    (B) sword : warrior
    (C) ink : pen
    (D) books : school bag
    (E) cannon : plunder

16. MACE : MAJESTY ::
    (A) king : crown
    (B) sword : soldier
    (C) diploma : knowledge
    (D) book : knowledge
    (E) house : security

17. VIXEN : SCOLD ::
    (A) wound : scar
    (B) hero : winner
    (C) bee : sting
    (D) pimple : irritate
    (E) duck : walk

18. DEBATE : SOLILOQUY ::
    (A) crowd : mob
    (B) Hamlet : Macbeth
    (C) Lincoln : Douglas
    (D) group : hermit
    (E) fight : defend

19. THREAT : INSECURITY ::
    (A) challenge : fight
    (B) reason : anger
    (C) thunder : lightning
    (D) speed : acceleration
    (E) discipline : learning

20. LARGE : ENORMOUS ::
    (A) cat : tiger
    (B) warmth : frost
    (C) plump : fat
    (D) royal : regal
    (E) happy : solemn

CORRECT ANSWERS

1. C	4. A	7. D	10. B	13. C	16. C	19. A
2. B	5. E	8. E	11. B	14. A	17. C	20. C
3. D	6. C	9. D	12. E	15. D	18. D	

EXPLANATORY ANSWERS TEST II. ANALOGY PAIRS

1. (C) ADVERSITY causes unhappiness, the opposite of HAPPINESS; VEHEMENCE causes conflict, the opposite of SERENITY.

2. (B) The LUTE is a STRING instrument just as the XYLOPHONE is a PERCUSSION instrument.

3. (D) One PLUCKs FEATHERS and SHEARs WOOL. The relationship is one of product to action involved in taking that product from an animal.

4. (A) MODESTY is the opposite of ARROGANCE; DEBILITY is the opposite of STRENGTH.

5. (E) When we BLOW on a HORN we produce a sound, just as when we TURN ON a RADIO.

6. (C) A BAY is smaller than a SEA and an extension of it, just as a PENINSULA is smaller than the LAND mass from which it protrudes. The relationship is one of part to whole.

7. (D) DECEMBER is the first month of WINTER; MARCH is the first month of SPRING.

8. (E) The key words, as well as all five choices, form a pair of synonymous adjectives in which the first adjective is stronger, or more intensive, than the second. However, PROFLIGATE is the best synonym for PRODIGAL and LAVISH is the best synonym for SPENDTHRIFT, making choice (E) the best answer.

9. (D) The AERIALIST uses a TRAPEZE in the performance of his work just as the MINER uses a PICK.

10. (B) When one SPEAKS at the wrong time, he might INTERRUPT; when one ENTERS at the wrong time, he might INTRUDE.

11. (B) ENCOURAGE is the opposite of RESTRICT. DEPRIVE is the opposite of SUPPLY.

12. (E) The key words are opposites as are answer choices (A), (C) and (E). BEFOUL is strongly negative in feeling, while TIDY is decidedly positive. Only INDICT : ACQUIT conveys the same negative-positive relationship.

13. (C) ITALY is the country where MILAN is located. Similarly, SPAIN is the country where MADRID is located.

14. (A) MIST is a minor kind of RAIN, just as WIND is a lesser kind of HURRICANE. The relationship is one of degree.

15. (D) A HOLSTER is used to carry a GUN; a SCHOOL BAG is used to carry BOOKS.

16. (C) A MACE is an ornamental staff borne as a symbol of authority or MAJESTY; a DIPLOMA is a symbol of educational achievement or the acquisition of KNOWLEDGE.

17. (C) A VIXEN attacks by SCOLDING; a BEE attacks by STINGING.

18. (D) A DEBATE is engaged in by two or more people; one person conducts a SOLILOQUY. A GROUP consists of several people; a HERMIT lives alone. The relationship is one of plural to singular.

19. (A) A THREAT often results in INSECURITY; a CHALLENGE often results in a FIGHT. The relationship is one of cause and effect.

20. (C) ENORMOUS means very LARGE; FAT means very PLUMP. The relationship is one of degree.

TEST III. ANALOGY PAIRS
TIME : 10 Minutes. 20 Questions.

Directions: Each of these test questions begins with two CAPITAL-IZED words which are related to each other in some way. Find out how they are related. Then study the five pairs of words that follow. They are lettered (A)(B)(C)(D)(E). Select the two words which are related to each other in the same way that the two CAPITALIZED words are related.

1. FIN : FISH ::
   (A) engine : auto
   (B) propeller : airplane
   (C) five : ten
   (D) teeth : stomach
   (E) leg : chair

2. RESTRAIN : REPRESS ::
   (A) advance : capitulate
   (B) surround : surrender
   (C) march : refrain
   (D) retire : battle
   (E) urge : spur

3. CONCERT : MUSIC ::
   (A) performance : artist
   (B) exhibition : art
   (C) play : actor
   (D) operetta : singer
   (E) flute : soloist

4. KEY : DOOR ::
   (A) combination : safe
   (B) keyhole : porthole
   (C) lock : key
   (D) opening : closing
   (E) bolt : safety

5. THROW : BOUNCE ::
   (A) carry : lift
   (B) drop : break
   (C) catch : hop
   (D) hold : miss
   (E) run : hide

6. AFTERNOON : DUSK ::
   (A) breakfast : dinner
   (B) yesterday : tomorrow
   (C) Sunday : Saturday
   (D) night : dawn
   (E) age : youth

7. STUDYING : LEARNING ::
   (A) running : jumping
   (B) investigating : discovering
   (C) reading : writing
   (D) dancing : singing
   (E) feeling : thinking

8. PULP : PAPER ::
   (A) rope : hemp
   (B) box : package
   (C) fabric : yarn
   (D) paper : package
   (E) cellulose : rayon

9. RUN : RACE ::
   (A) walk : pogo stick
   (B) swim : boat
   (C) fly : kite
   (D) sink : bottle
   (E) repair : automobile

10. OBSTRUCTION : BUOY ::
    (A) construction : building
    (B) boy : girl
    (C) danger : red light
    (D) iceberg : titanic
    (E) barricade : wall

11. EXPEDITE : HASTEN ::
    (A) illuminate : disturb
    (B) refine : refute
    (C) inflate : distend
    (D) scour : squeeze
    (E) augment : lessen

12. VIBRATION : SOUND ::
    (A) gravity : pull
    (B) watercolor : paint
    (C) accident : death
    (D) worm : reptile
    (E) drought : plague

13. WRITE : LETTER ::
    (A) pen : paper
    (B) drink : glass
    (C) act : part
    (D) rhyme : poem
    (E) memorize : book

14. DEPRESSION : MASO-CHISM ::
    (A) man : animal
    (B) one : many
    (C) psychiatry : cure
    (D) revenge : sadism
    (E) greed : avarice

15. SKIN : MAN ::
    (A) scaled : fur
    (B) hide : hair
    (C) walls : room
    (D) window : house
    (E) clothes : lady

16. ELIXIR : PILL ::
    (A) life : health
    (B) water : ice
    (C) bottle : box
    (D) mystery : medicine
    (E) nurse : doctor

17. FRUGAL : ECONOMICAL ::
    (A) fragile : solid
    (B) prosperous : wealthy
    (C) fruitful : sunny
    (D) regal : comical
    (E) spendthrift : miser

18. MUNDANE : TEMPORAL ::
    (A) earthly : heavenly
    (B) celestial : starry
    (C) spiritual : everlasting
    (D) angelic : religious
    (E) ephemeral : eternal

19. CLARINET : MUSIC ::
    (A) symbol : sign
    (B) chalk : writing
    (C) daughter : father
    (D) pencil : pen
    (E) bread : flour

20. FURIOUS : ANGRY ::
    (A) cold : frozen
    (B) love : like
    (C) embrace : hug
    (D) slap : hit
    (E) wish : fulfillment

CORRECT ANSWERS

1.	B	4.	A	7.	B	10.	C	13.	C	16.	B	19.	B
2.	E	5.	B	8.	E	11.	C	14.	D	17.	B	20.	B
3.	B	6.	D	9.	C	12.	A	15.	C	18.	C		

EXPLANATORY ANSWERS TEST III. ANALOGY PAIRS

1. (B) A FIN propels a FISH; a PROPELLER propels an AIRPLANE.

2. (E) RESTRAIN and REPRESS are synonyms, as are URGE and SPUR.

3. You hear MUSIC at a CONCERT; you see ART at an EXHIBITION.

4. (A) The right KEY opens the DOOR; the right COMBINATION opens the SAFE.

5. (B) If you THROW a certain type of object (like a rubber ball) at a solid surface, it may BOUNCE. If you DROP a certain type of object (like an egg) on a solid surface, it may BREAK.

6. (D) In this sequence relationship, AFTERNOON precedes DUSK as NIGHT precedes DAWN.

7. (B) STUDYING is required for LEARNING; INVESTIGATING is required for DISCOVERING.

8. (E) PULP is used in making PAPER; CELLULOSE is used in making RAYON.

9. (C) One RUNS a RACE and FLIES a KITE. The relationship is one of action to object.

10. (C) A BUOY warns of an OBSTRUCTION; a RED LIGHT warns of DANGER.

11. (C) EXPEDITE and HASTEN are synonyms, as are INFLATE and DISTEND.

12. (A) SOUND is caused by VIBRATION; PULL is caused by GRAVITY. The relationship is one of cause and effect.

13. (C) One WRITES a LETTER and ACTS a PART in this action-to-object relationship.

14. (D) DEPRESSION and MASOCHISM refer to pain or injury to oneself; REVENGE and SADISM refer to pain or injury to another.

15. (C) SKIN encloses a MAN; WALLS enclose a ROOM.

16. (B) An ELIXIR is a liquid medicine; a PILL is a solid medicine. WATER is liquid; ICE is solid.

17. (B) FRUGAL and ECONOMICAL are synonyms, as are PROSPEROUS and WEALTHY.

18. (C) What is MUNDANE is usually considered TEMPORAL; what is SPIRITUAL is usually considered EVERLASTING.

19. (B) A CLARINET is used to produce MUSIC; CHALK is used for WRITING.

20. (B) Being FURIOUS is a more intense emotion than being ANGRY; LOVE is a more intense emotion than LIKE. The relationship is one of degree.

TEST IV. ANALOGY PAIRS
TIME: 10 Minutes. 20 Questions.

Directions: Each of these test questions begins with two CAPITALIZED words which are related to each other in some way. Find out how they are related. Then study the five pairs of words that follow. They are lettered (A)(B)(C)(D)(E). Select the two words which are related to each other in the same way that the two CAPITALIZED words are related.

1. RAIN : DROPS
   (A) ice : winter
   (B) cloud : sky
   (C) flake : snow
   (D) ocean : stream
   (E) mankind : man

2. SCHOOL : LEARN ::
   (A) book : read
   (B) wheel : tire
   (C) knife : bread
   (D) press : print
   (E) teacher : learn

3. HORSE : CENTAUR ::
   (A) stable : barn
   (B) decade : century
   (C) pig : sty
   (D) fish : mermaid
   (E) hydra : chimera

4. MODEST : QUIET ::
   (A) cynical : determined
   (B) conceited : loquacious
   (C) capable : stubborn
   (D) egocentric : reserved
   (E) demure ; brash

5. IMPORTANT : CRUCIAL ::
   (A) orange : lemon
   (B) sorrow : death
   (C) misdemeanor : felony
   (D) poverty : uncleanliness
   (E) axiom : hypothesis

6. WATER : SWIMMING
   (A) egg : breaking
   (B) fire : flaming
   (C) chair : sitting
   (D) learning : knowledge
   (E) deed: owning

7. TOWER : CASTLE ::
   (A) car : motor
   (B) grass : prairie
   (C) house : chimney
   (D) rider : horse
   (E) dungeon : sepulcher

8. WANTON : SAINT ::
   (A) prolific : bounteous
   (B) kindly : stingy
   (C) atheistic : priest
   (D) stolid : stoic
   (E) capitalistic : anapest

9. PEOPLE : ELECT ::
   (A) statesman : govern
   (B) lawyer : debate
   (C) teach : teacher
   (D) diplomat : argue
   (E) journalist : news

10. JUSTICE : SCALES ::
    (A) ruler : education
    (B) weathervane : cock
    (C) tree : farm
    (D) court : crime
    (E) pearl : wisdom

11. UXORIOUS : MISOGY-
    NOUS ::
    (A) philanthropic : charitable
    (B) useless : mystic
    (C) satanic : angelic
    (D) tender : gracious
    (E) domestic : national

12. RULE : KINGDOM ::
    (A) starvation : famine
    (B) oppression : serfdom
    (C) proof : reason
    (D) reign : ruler
    (E) discipline : children

13. UNFRIENDLY : HOSTILE ::
    (A) weak : ill
    (B) weak : strong
    (C) blaze : flame
    (D) useful : necessary
    (E) violence : danger

14. PAMPHLET : BOOK ::
    (A) dress : sweater
    (B) discomfort : pain
    (C) height : weight
    (D) swimming : wading
    (E) epilogue : summary

15. CONSTELLATION: STARS ::
    (A) state : country
    (B) library : book
    (C) archipelago : islands
    (D) continent : peninsula
    (E) dollar : penny

16. CALIBRATOR : MEASURE ::
    (A) plumber : wrench
    (B) clamp : hold
    (C) ruler : line
    (D) measure : tolerance
    (E) thermometer : temperature

17. PAPER : REAM ::
    (A) eggs : dozen
    (B) newspaper : stand
    (C) apartment : room
    (D) candy : wrapper
    (E) gaggle : geese

18. SAIL : SALE ::
    (A) cat : rat
    (B) blue : blew
    (C) tar : car
    (D) flew : flaw
    (E) hug : huge

19. SHAKESPEARE : IBSEN ::
    (A) Tolstoy : Keats
    (B) Aeschylus : Albee
    (C) Dickens : Milton
    (D) Joyce : Chaucer
    (E) Shaw : Hawthorne

20. GOOD FRIDAY : CHRIST-
    MAS ::
    (A) opening : closing
    (B) holiday : school
    (C) end : beginning
    (D) New Year : Christmas
    (E) crucifixion : resurrection

CORRECT ANSWERS

1.	E	4.	B	7.	D	10.	B	13.	C	16.	B	19.	B
2.	D	5.	C	8.	C	11.	C	14.	B	17.	A	20.	C
3.	D	6.	C	9.	A	12.	E	15.	C	18.	B		

EXPLANATORY ANSWERS TEST IV. ANALOGY PAIRS

1. (E) RAIN is made up of DROPS; MANKIND is made up of MEN. The relationship is that of whole to part.

2. (D) The purpose of a SCHOOL is to LEARN; the purpose of a PRESS is to PRINT.

3. (D) A CENTAUR has as its upper part a man and as its lower part a HORSE; a MERMAID is part woman and part FISH. Both a centaur and a mermaid are legendary. The relationship is that of a component part to the whole legendary creature.

4. (B) A MODEST person is usually QUIET; a CONCEITED person is usually LOQUACIOUS. The relationship is one of ASSOCIATION.

5. (C) In this analogy of degree, something that is CRUCIAL is very IMPORTANT; a FELONY is a more serious offense than a MISDEMEANOR.

6. (C) WATER might be used for SWIMMING. A CHAIR is usually used for SITTING. Note that water and chair are both concrete nouns. The relationship is one of medium or implement to its associated use.

7. (D) A TOWER is atop a CASTLE; a RIDER is atop a HORSE. Choices (A) (B) (C) and (E) do not convey this relationship.

8. (C) The relationship between the key words—"If you are A you are not B"—exists only in choices (B) and (C). However, only choice (C) is in the relationship of adjective:noun as established by the key word pair.

9. (A) PEOPLE are known to ELECT and STATESMEN are known to GOVERN. The relationship is that of a particular group to its associated activity.

10. (B) We associate JUSTICE with SCALES. We associate a WEATHERVANE with a COCK; in fact, a weathervane is often called a weathercock.

11. (C) UXORIOUS and MISOGYNOUS are opposites, as are SATANIC and ANGELIC.

12. (E) We speak of the RULE (control) of a KINGDOM and the DISCIPLINE (control) of CHILDREN. The relationship is one of association.

13. (C) UNFRIENDLY and HOSTILE are synonyms, as are BLAZE and FLAME.

14. (B) A PAMPHLET is a short printed work; a BOOK is longer. DISCOMFORT is a milder form of PAIN. The relationship is one of degree.

15. (C) A group of STARS make up a CONSTELLATION; a group of ISLANDS make up an ARCHIPELAGO. The relationship is that of whole to part.

16. (B) A CALIBRATOR is used to MEASURE; a CLAMP is used to HOLD. The relationship is one of tool to function.

17. (A) PAPER is counted by the REAM; EGGS are counted by the DOZEN. The relationship is one of item to unit of measure.

18. (B) SAIL-SALE and BLUE-BLEW are homophone pairs, or homonyms. A homophone is a word identical with another in pronunciation but differing in spelling and meaning.

19. (B) SHAKESPEARE, IBSEN, AESCHYLUS, and ALBEE are all playwrights. Foils A, C, D and E are not all playwrights.

20. GOOD FRIDAY commemorates the death of Christ; CHRISTMAS commemorates the birth of Christ. The answer hinges on the relationship of end to beginning.

TEST V. ANALOGY PAIRS
TIME : 10 Minutes. 20 Questions.

Directions: Each of these test questions begins with two CAPITAL-IZED words which are related to each other in some way. Find out how they are related. Then study the five pairs of words that follow. They are lettered (A) (B) (C) (D) (E). Select the two words which are related to each other in the same way that the two CAPITALIZED words are related.

1. APPRENTICE:CRAFTS-MAN::
   (A) reporter : editor
   (B) lawyer : judge
   (C) boy : man
   (D) typist : stenographer
   (E) student : teacher

2. AUTHOR : NOVEL ::
   (A) teacher : student
   (B) reader : interest
   (C) hero : conquest
   (D) carpenter : cabinet
   (E) doctor : cure

3. SELL : PURCHASE ::
   (A) pay : charge
   (B) eager : anxious
   (C) gift : earned
   (D) sale : sold
   (E) give : receive

4. AMENITIES : GENTLEMEN ::
   (A) regulations : player
   (B) society : lady
   (C) profanity : hobo
   (D) requirements : professor
   (E) media : journalist

5. MEDICINE : SCIENCE ::
   (A) daughter : father
   (B) tomato : fruit
   (C) penicillin : aspirin
   (D) school : college
   (E) mammal : reptile

6. AIMLESSNESS : DELIN-
   QUENCY ::
   (A) aggression : appeasement
   (B) belligerence : mischief
   (C) slum : dirt
   (D) boredom : mischief
   (E) crime : vandalism

7. SADIST : INJURY ::
   (A) dentist : teeth
   (B) thief : robbery
   (C) priest : church
   (D) pupil : desk
   (E) opportunist : generosity

8. RUBBER : FLEXIBILITY ::
   (A) iron : pliability
   (B) wood : plastic
   (C) steel : rigidity
   (D) iron : elasticity
   (E) synthetics : natural

9. CITIZEN : CONSTITUTION ::
   (A) alien : consul
   (B) emigrant : passport
   (C) resident : law
   (D) immigrant : visa
   (E) union : laborer

10. RECKLESSNESS : VALOR ::
    (A) courage : cowardice
    (B) reliance : dependability
    (C) restitution : confirmation
    (D) usury : interest
    (E) conservation : ecology

11. WICKED : SCORN ::
    (A) commendable : emulate
    (B) devilish : revere
    (C) celebrated : exculpate
    (D) weak : oust
    (E) honor : award

12. BELL : RING ::
    (A) clock : build
    (B) alarm : sound
    (C) light : switch
    (D) scissors : handle
    (E) bicycle : ride

13. BOY : MAN ::
    (A) wall : floor
    (B) calf : cow
    (C) seat : chair
    (D) knob : door
    (E) history : legend

14. PINK : RED ::
    (A) chartreuse : green
    (B) blue : turquoise
    (C) blue : pink
    (D) yellow : white
    (E) gray : beige

15. ABSENCE : PRESENCE ::
    (A) steady : secure
    (B) poor : influential
    (C) fresh : salted
    (D) safe : influential
    (E) stable : changeable

16. LAW : PROSECUTOR ::
    (A) constitution : attorney general
    (B) Congress : President
    (C) legislation : governor
    (D) Bible : minister
    (E) athletics : boxer

17. RABBIT'S FOOT : FOUR-
    LEAF CLOVER ::
    (A) wishing well : pennies
    (B) devil : Satan
    (C) 13 : black cat
    (D) horseshoe : horse
    (E) 7 : white cat

18. SYMPATHY : ADVERSITY ::
    (A) acceptance : pathos
    (B) happiness : sadness
    (C) suppression : emotion
    (D) condolences : grief
    (E) innocence : guilt

19. FLUID : LIGHTER ::
    (A) wood : pencil
    (B) gas : automobile
    (C) chair : table
    (D) dust : chalk
    (E) oil : lubrication

20. POSSIBLE : PROBABLE ::
    (A) likely : unlikely
    (B) best : better
    (C) willing : anxious
    (D) quick : fast
    (E) frighten : worry

CORRECT ANSWERS

1. E	4. A	7. B	10. D	13. B	16. A	19. B
2. D	5. B	8. C	11. A	14. A	17. C	20. C
3. E	6. D	9. C	12. B	15. E	18. D	

EXPLANATORY ANSWERS TEST V. ANALOGY PAIRS

1. (E) A CRAFTSMAN guides an APPRENTICE as he or she learns a trade. A TEACHER guides a STUDENT as he or she learns a subject.

2. (D) An AUTHOR writes a NOVEL; a CARPENTER builds a CABINET. The relationship is that of worker to product.

3. (E) One SELLs an item to another who thereby PURCHASEs it. One GIVEs an item to another who thereby RECEIVEs it.

4. (A) A GENTLEMAN is supposed to observe the social AMENITIES; a PLAYER is supposed to observe the REGULATIONS.

5. (B) MEDICINE is one SCIENCE; a TOMATO is one FRUIT. The relationship is that of part to whole.

6. (D) AIMLESSNESS often leads to DELINQUENCY; BOREDOM often leads to MISCHIEF. The relationship is one of cause and effect.

7. (B) A SADIST commits INJURY to others: a THIEF commits ROBBERY.

8. (C) One characteristic of RUBBER is FLEXIBILITY; one characeristic of STEEL is RIGIDITY.

9. (C) A CITIZEN is bound by the CONSTITUTION, just as a RESIDENT is bound by the LAW.

10. (D) Uncontrolled VALOR may result in RECKLESSNESS, just as uncontrolled INTEREST rates may result in USURY.

11. (A) We should SCORN what is WICKED; we should EMULATE what is COMMENDABLE.

12. (B) In creating sound, we may RING a BELL or SOUND an ALARM.

13. (B) A BOY becomes a MAN and a CALF becomes a COW.

14. (A) PINK is a pale RED; CHARTREUSE is a pale GREEN.

15. **(E)** ABSENCE and PRESENCE are opposites, as are STABLE and CHANGEABLE.

16. **(A)** The PROSECUTOR sees to it that the LAW is obeyed; the ATTORNEY GENERAL sees to it that the CONSTITUTION is obeyed.

17. **(C)** The RABBIT'S FOOT and the FOUR-LEAF CLOVER are symbols of good luck. Conversely, the number 13 and the BLACK CAT are symbols of bad luck.

18. **(D)** We give SYMPATHY to a person who experiences ADVERSITY; we give CONDOLENCES to a person who experiences GRIEF.

19. **(B)** We put FLUID into a LIGHTER to make it work; we put GASOLINE into an AUTOMOBILE to make it go.

20. **(C)** Something that is POSSIBLE might be, but is not necessarily, PROBABLE. Someone who is WILLING might be, but is not necessarily, ANXIOUS.

TEST VI. ANALOGY PAIRS
TIME: 25 Minutes. 50 Questions.

Directions: Each of these test questions begins with two CAPITALIZED words which are related to each other in some way. Find out how they are related. Then study the five pairs of words that follow. They are lettered (A) (B) (C) (D) (E). Select the two words which are related to each other in the same way that the two CAPITALIZED words are related.

1. HAIR : BALD ::
   (A) wig : head
   (B) egg : eggshell
   (C) rain : drought
   (D) skin : scar
   (E) healthy : sick

2. BOAT : SHIP ::
   (A) book : volume
   (B) canoe : paddle
   (C) oar : water
   (D) aft : stern
   (E) land : sea

3. SCYTHE : DEATH ::
   (A) fall : winter
   (B) knife : murder
   (C) sickle : grain
   (D) harvest : crops
   (E) arrow : love

4. CARNIVORE : ANIMALS ::
   (A) omnivore : omelets
   (B) vegetarian : vegetables
   (C) trace : minerals
   (D) herbivore : healthy
   (E) pollination : plants

5. MAUVE : COLOR ::
   (A) basil : spice
   (B) colorless : colored
   (C) light : dark
   (D) tan : brown
   (E) blue : rainbow

6. MUFFLE : SILENCE ::
   (A) cover : bell
   (D) sound : hearing
   (C) cry : loud
   (D) stymie : defeat
   (E) glimpse : look

7. DEARTH : PAUCITY ::
   (A) few : many
   (B) scarcity : shortage
   (C) shortage : plethora
   (D) empty : container
   (E) commodity : expectation

8. WATERMARK : BIRTH-
   MARK ::
   (A) buoy : stamp
   (B) paper : person
   (C) tide : character
   (D) line : signal
   (E) meaning : significance

9. BRIGHT : BRILLIANT ::
   (A) color : red
   (B) yellow : red
   (C) window : light
   (D) light : fire
   (E) happy : ecstatic

10. POWERFUL : MIGHTY ::
    (A) muscle : boxer
    (B) same : alike
    (C) strength : exercise
    (D) weak : small
    (E) great : bigger

11. NEWS REPORT : DESCRIP-
    TIVE ::
    (A) weather report : unpre-
        dictable
    (B) editorial : one-sided
    (C) feature story : newsworthy
    (D) commercial : prescriptive
    (E) joke : funny

12. AGREEMENT:CONSENSUS::
    (A) count : census
    (B) pleasure : enjoy
    (C) peace : tranquility
    (D) argument : solution
    (E) action : incite

13. WATER : HYDRAULIC ::
    (A) energy : atomic

(B) power : electric
(C) gasoline : combustion
(D) pressure : compress
(E) air : pneumatic

14. STABLE : HORSE ::
    (A) barn : cow
    (B) sty : pig
    (C) fold : ram
    (D) coop : hen
    (E) zoo : lioness

15. ROLE : ACTOR ::
    (A) aria : soprano
    (B) private : soldier
    (C) melody : singer
    (D) position : ballplayer
    (E) character : part

16. PROW : SHIP ::
    (A) snout : hog
    (B) nose : airplane
    (C) bird : beak
    (D) wheel : car
    (E) point : shaft

17. MAXIMUM : MINIMUM ::
    (A) pessimist : optimist
    (B) minimum : optimum
    (C) best : good
    (D) most : least
    (E) wane : wax

18. SENSATION:ANESTHETIC::
    (A) breath : lung
    (B) drug : reaction
    (C) satisfaction:disappointment
    (D) poison : antidote
    (E) observation : sight

19. DISEMBARK : SHIP ::
    (A) board : train
    (B) dismount : horse
    (C) intern : jail
    (D) discharge : navy
    (E) dismantle : clock

20. PROTEIN : MEAT ::
(A) calories : cream
(B) energy : sugar
(C) cyclamates : diet
(D) starch : potatoes
(E) fat : cholesterol

21. NECK : NAPE ::
(A) foot : heel
(B) head : forehead
(C) arm : wrist
(D) stomach : back
(E) eye : lid

22. GRIPPING : PLIERS ::
(A) chisel : gouging
(B) breaking : hammer
(C) elevating : jack
(D) killing : knife
(E) fastening : screwdriver

23. RADIUS : CIRCLE ::
(A) rubber : tire
(B) bisect : angle
(C) equator : earth
(D) cord : circumference
(E) spoke : wheel

24. HAIR : HORSE ::
(A) feather : bird
(B) wool : sheep
(C) down : pillow
(D) peach : fuzz
(E) fur : animal

25. GOBBLE : TURKEY ::
(A) poison : cobra
(B) bark : tree
(C) trunk : elephant
(D) twitter : bird
(E) king : lion

26. ASTUTE : STUPID ::
(A) scholar : idiotic
(B) agile : clumsy
(C) lonely : clown
(D) dance : ignorant
(E) intelligent : smart

27. WHALE : FISH ::
(A) collie : dog
(B) fly : insect
(C) bat : bird
(D) clue : detective
(E) mako : shark

28. GOLD : PROSPECTOR ::
(A) medicine : doctor
(B) prayer : preacher
(C) wood : carpenter
(D) clue : detective
(E) iron : machinist

29. COUPLET : POEM ::
(A) page : letter
(B) sentence : paragraph
(C) number : address
(D) epic : poetry
(E) biography : novel

30. OIL : WELL ::
(A) water : faucet
(B) iron : ore
(C) silver : mine
(D) gas : tank
(E) lumber : yard

31. RUDDER : SHIP ::
(A) wheel : car
(B) motor : truck
(C) row : boat
(D) kite : string
(E) wing : plane

32. STALLION : ROOSTER ::
(A) buck : doe
(B) filly : colt
(C) horse : chicken
(D) foal : calf
(E) mare : hen

33. READ : BOOK ::
(A) taste : salty
(B) attend : movie
(C) smell : odor
(D) listen : record
(E) touch : paper

34. PARROT : SPARROW ::
    (A) dog : poodle
    (B) elephant : ant
    (C) goldfish : guppy
    (D) lion : cat
    (E) eagle : butterly

35. BONES : LIGAMENT ::
    (A) break : stretch
    (B) muscles : tendon
    (C) fat : cell
    (D) knuckle : finger
    (E) knee : joint

36. SPICY : INSIPID ::
    (A) pepper : salt
    (B) hot : creamy
    (C) exciting : dull
    (D) cucumber : pickle
    (E) bland : sharp

37. BURL : TREE ::
    (A) silver : ore
    (B) bronze : copper
    (C) plank : wood
    (D) glass : sand
    (E) pearl : oyster

38. YEAST : LEAVEN ::
    (A) soda : bubble
    (B) iodine : antiseptic
    (C) aspirin : medicine
    (D) flour : dough
    (E) penicillin : plant

39. NUMEROUS : POLYGON ::
    (A) circumference : circle
    (B) hypotenuse : triangle
    (C) point : line
    (D) degree : angle
    (E) four : square

40. EXPURGATE : PASSAGES ::
    (A) defoliate : leaves
    (B) cancel : checks
    (C) incorporate : ideas
    (D) invade : privacy
    (E) till : fields

41. PHARMACIST : DRUGS ::
    (A) psychiatrist : ideas
    (B) mentor : drills
    (C) mechanic : troubles
    (D) chef : foods
    (E) nurse : diseases

42. CONQUER : SUBJUGATE ::
    (A) esteem : respect
    (B) slander : vilify
    (C) discern : observe
    (D) ponder : deliberate
    (E) freedom : slavery

43. ENGRAVING : CHISEL ::
    (A) printing : paper
    (B) photography : camera
    (C) lithography : stone
    (D) printing : ink
    (E) etching : acid

44. DECIBEL : SOUND ::
    (A) calorie : weight
    (B) volt : electricity
    (C) temperature : weather
    (D) color : light
    (E) area : distance

45. HOMONYM : SOUND ::
    (A) synonym : same
    (B) antonym : meaning
    (C) acronym : ideas
    (D) pseudonym : fake
    (E) synopsis : summary

46. CHAIR : FURNITURE ::
    (A) tire : rubber
    (B) tree : plant
    (C) food : meat
    (D) boat : float
    (E) car : transport

47. VALUELESS : INVALU-ABLE ::
    (A) miserly : philanthropic
    (B) frugality : wealth
    (C) thriftiness : cheap
    (D) costly : cut-rate
    (E) cheap : unsalable

48. TRIANGLE : PRISM ::
    (A) sphere : earth
    (B) square : rhomboid
    (C) rectangle : building
    (D) circle : cylinder
    (E) polygon : diamond

49. YOKE : OX ::
    (A) saddle : stallion
    (B) tether : cow

    (C) herd : sheep
    (D) brand : steer
    (E) harness : horse

50. COW : BUTTER ::
    (A) chicken : omelets
    (B) tree : fruit
    (C) steer : mutton
    (D) water : ice
    (E) grape : raisin

CORRECT ANSWERS

1.	C	11.	D	21.	A	31.	A	41.	D
2.	A	12.	C	22.	C	32.	E	42.	B
3.	E	13.	E	23.	E	33.	D	43.	E
4.	B	14.	B	24.	B	34.	C	44.	B
5.	A	15.	D	25.	D	35.	B	45.	B
6.	D	16.	B	26.	B	36.	C	46.	B
7.	B	17.	D	27.	C	37.	E	47.	A
8.	B	18.	D	28.	D	38.	B	48.	D
9.	E	19.	B	29.	B	39.	E	49.	E
10.	B	20.	D	30.	C	40.	A	50.	A

EXPLANATORY ANSWERS TEST VI. ANALOGY PAIRS

1. (C) To be BALD is to lack HAIR. In a DROUGHT there is a lack of RAIN.

2. (A) A SHIP is more than just an ordinary BOAT, and a VOLUME is more than just an ordinary BOOK.

3. (E) A SCYTHE is involved in symbolizing DEATH, as an ARROW is in symbolizing LOVE.

4. (B) A CARNIVORE eats ANIMALS; a VEGETARIAN eats VEGETABLES.

5. (A) MAUVE is a COLOR, and BASIL is a SPICE.

6. (D) To MUFFLE something is almost to SILENCE it. To STYMIE something is almost to DEFEAT it.

7. (B) PAUCITY is a synonym for DEARTH, and SHORTAGE for SCARCITY.

8. (B) PAPER is sometimes identified by a WATERMARK, and a PERSON by a BIRTHMARK.

9. (E) A person who is extremely BRIGHT is BRILLIANT. A person who is extremely HAPPY is ECSTATIC.

10. (B) Those who are POWER-FUL are also MIGHTY. Things that are the SAME are also ALIKE.

11. (D) A NEWS REPORT is DESCRIPTIVE of an event, but a COMMERCIAL is PRE-SCRIPTIVE, recommending rather than describing.

12. (C) In a case of CONSENSUS among individuals, there is ne-cessarily AGREEMENT. Where there is TRANQUILITY among individuals, there is necessarily PEACE.

13. (E) HYDRAULIC describes something that is operated by means of WATER; PNEU-MATIC describes something that is operated by means of AIR.

14. (B) A HORSE is usually kept and fed in a STABLE; a PIG is usually kept and fed in a STY. The parallel to horse and pig would be chicken, not hen.

15. (D) The ACTOR plays a ROLE, as a BALLPLAYER plays a POSITION.

16. (B) The PROW is the forward part of the SHIP, as the NOSE is the forward part of the AIRPLANE.

17. (D) MAXIMUM and MINI-MUM mark extremes in quan-tity, as do MOST and LEAST.

18. (D) One can counteract a SEN-SATION with an ANESTHET-IC and a POISON with an ANTIDOTE.

19. (B) One leaves a SHIP by DIS-EMBARKING and a HORSE by DISMOUNTING.

20. (D) MEAT is a food that sup-plies us with PROTEIN; POTA-TOES are a food that supplies us with STARCH.

21. (A) The NAPE is the back of the NECK, and the HEEL is the back of the FOOT.

22. (C) PLIERS are designed for GRIPPING, and a JACK, for ELEVATING.

23. (E) The RADIUS moves from the center of the CIRCLE to the edge, as the SPOKE moves from the center of the WHEEL to the edge.

24. (B) A HORSE is a four-legged animal that is covered with HAIR. A SHEEP is a four-legged animal that is covered with WOOL.

25. (D) A GOBBLE is a sound made by a particular kind of bird, a TURKEY. A TWITTER is a sound made by some BIRDS.

26. (B) As ASTUTE is in emphatic opposition to STUPID, so is AGILE in opposition to CLUMSY. Both terms go be-yond simple denials of the op-posing terms.

27. (C) A WHALE is a mammal that is mistakenly thought to be a FISH, and a BAT is a mammal that is mistakenly thought to be a BIRD.

28. (D) A PROSPECTOR seeks GOLD, and a DETECTIVE seeks a CLUE.

29. (B) A COUPLET makes up part of a POEM, and a SENTENCE makes up part of a PARAGRAPH.

30. (C) OIL is extracted from the earth by means of a WELL, and SILVER by means of a MINE.

31. (A) A RUDDER is used in directing a SHIP. A WHEEL is used in directing a CAR.

32. (E) A STALLION and a ROOSTER are two different animals of the same sex, as are a MARE and a HEN.

33. (D) We assimilate a BOOK through READING, and a RECORD through LISTENING.

34. (C) A PARROT and a SPARROW are two very different sorts of birds. A GOLDFISH and a GUPPY are two very different sorts of fish.

35. (B) MUSCLES are connected to bone by TENDONS just as BONES are connected to bones by LIGAMENTS.

36. (C) Food that is INSIPID is DULL and uninteresting, whereas SPICY food can be said to be EXCITING.

37. (E) A BURL is an outgrowth of a TREE, and a PEARL is an outgrowth of an OYSTER.

38. (B) YEAST is used as a LEAVEN, and IODINE as an ANTI-SEPTIC. These functions are more specific than aspirin's function as a medicine.

39. (E) A POLYGON has NUMEROUS sides. A SQUARE has FOUR sides.

40. (A) One can EXPURGATE (eliminate) PASSAGES as one can DEFOLIATE LEAVES.

41. (D) The basic materials of a PHARMACIST are DRUGS; the basic materials of a CHEF are FOODS.

42. (B) To CONQUER someone is to SUBJUGATE him. To SLANDER someone is to VILIFY him. In both cases, the subject is hostile toward the object.

43. (E) A CHISEL can be used to cut out an ENGRAVING. ACID can be used to cut through a surface to create an ETCHING.

44. (B) SOUND is measured in DECIBELS. and ELECTRICITY in VOLTS.

45. (B) SOUND determines whether two words are HOMONYMS. MEANING determines whether two words are ANTONYMS.

46. (B) A CHAIR is a piece of FURNITURE and a TREE is an individual PLANT.

47. (A) At one extreme something can be VALUELESS, and at another extreme something can be INVALUABLE. At one extreme an individual can be

MISERLY, and at another extreme, PHILANTHROPIC.

48. (D) A TRIANGLE has three sides, and a PRISM is a three-sided solid figure. A CIRCLE is circular, and CYLINDER is a solid figure that is circular.

49. (E) An OX is controlled by means of a YOKE. A HORSE is controlled by means of a HARNESS.

50. (A) Both a COW and a CHICKEN are animals. Indirectly, BUTTER is a product from the former and OMELETS are products from the latter.

VERBAL ANALOGIES TEST I. SYNONYMS

1 Ⓐ Ⓑ Ⓒ Ⓓ   6 Ⓐ Ⓑ Ⓒ Ⓓ   11 Ⓐ Ⓑ Ⓒ Ⓓ   16 Ⓐ Ⓑ Ⓒ Ⓓ   21 Ⓐ Ⓑ Ⓒ Ⓓ

2 Ⓐ Ⓑ Ⓒ Ⓓ   7 Ⓐ Ⓑ Ⓒ Ⓓ   12 Ⓐ Ⓑ Ⓒ Ⓓ   17 Ⓐ Ⓑ Ⓒ Ⓓ   22 Ⓐ Ⓑ Ⓒ Ⓓ

3 Ⓐ Ⓑ Ⓒ Ⓓ   8 Ⓐ Ⓑ Ⓒ Ⓓ   13 Ⓐ Ⓑ Ⓒ Ⓓ   18 Ⓐ Ⓑ Ⓒ Ⓓ   23 Ⓐ Ⓑ Ⓒ Ⓓ

4 Ⓐ Ⓑ Ⓒ Ⓓ   9 Ⓐ Ⓑ Ⓒ Ⓓ   14 Ⓐ Ⓑ Ⓒ Ⓓ   19 Ⓐ Ⓑ Ⓒ Ⓓ   24 Ⓐ Ⓑ Ⓒ Ⓓ

5 Ⓐ Ⓑ Ⓒ Ⓓ   10 Ⓐ Ⓑ Ⓒ Ⓓ   15 Ⓐ Ⓑ Ⓒ Ⓓ   20 Ⓐ Ⓑ Ⓒ Ⓓ   25 Ⓐ Ⓑ Ⓒ Ⓓ

   26 Ⓐ Ⓑ Ⓒ Ⓓ

VERBAL ANALOGIES TEST II. ANTONYMS

1 Ⓐ Ⓑ Ⓒ Ⓓ   6 Ⓐ Ⓑ Ⓒ Ⓓ   11 Ⓐ Ⓑ Ⓒ Ⓓ   16 Ⓐ Ⓑ Ⓒ Ⓓ   21 Ⓐ Ⓑ Ⓒ Ⓓ

2 Ⓐ Ⓑ Ⓒ Ⓓ   7 Ⓐ Ⓑ Ⓒ Ⓓ   12 Ⓐ Ⓑ Ⓒ Ⓓ   17 Ⓐ Ⓑ Ⓒ Ⓓ   22 Ⓐ Ⓑ Ⓒ Ⓓ

3 Ⓐ Ⓑ Ⓒ Ⓓ   8 Ⓐ Ⓑ Ⓒ Ⓓ   13 Ⓐ Ⓑ Ⓒ Ⓓ   18 Ⓐ Ⓑ Ⓒ Ⓓ   23 Ⓐ Ⓑ Ⓒ Ⓓ

4 Ⓐ Ⓑ Ⓒ Ⓓ   9 Ⓐ Ⓑ Ⓒ Ⓓ   14 Ⓐ Ⓑ Ⓒ Ⓓ   19 Ⓐ Ⓑ Ⓒ Ⓓ   24 Ⓐ Ⓑ Ⓒ Ⓓ

5 Ⓐ Ⓑ Ⓒ Ⓓ   10 Ⓐ Ⓑ Ⓒ Ⓓ   15 Ⓐ Ⓑ Ⓒ Ⓓ   20 Ⓐ Ⓑ Ⓒ Ⓓ   25 Ⓐ Ⓑ Ⓒ Ⓓ

   26 Ⓐ Ⓑ Ⓒ Ⓓ

VERBAL ANALOGIES TEST III. CAUSE AND EFFECT

1 Ⓐ Ⓑ Ⓒ Ⓓ   6 Ⓐ Ⓑ Ⓒ Ⓓ   11 Ⓐ Ⓑ Ⓒ Ⓓ   16 Ⓐ Ⓑ Ⓒ Ⓓ   21 Ⓐ Ⓑ Ⓒ Ⓓ

2 Ⓐ Ⓑ Ⓒ Ⓓ   7 Ⓐ Ⓑ Ⓒ Ⓓ   12 Ⓐ Ⓑ Ⓒ Ⓓ   17 Ⓐ Ⓑ Ⓒ Ⓓ   22 Ⓐ Ⓑ Ⓒ Ⓓ

3 Ⓐ Ⓑ Ⓒ Ⓓ   8 Ⓐ Ⓑ Ⓒ Ⓓ   13 Ⓐ Ⓑ Ⓒ Ⓓ   18 Ⓐ Ⓑ Ⓒ Ⓓ   23 Ⓐ Ⓑ Ⓒ Ⓓ

4 Ⓐ Ⓑ Ⓒ Ⓓ   9 Ⓐ Ⓑ Ⓒ Ⓓ   14 Ⓐ Ⓑ Ⓒ Ⓓ   19 Ⓐ Ⓑ Ⓒ Ⓓ   24 Ⓐ Ⓑ Ⓒ Ⓓ

5 Ⓐ Ⓑ Ⓒ Ⓓ   10 Ⓐ Ⓑ Ⓒ Ⓓ   15 Ⓐ Ⓑ Ⓒ Ⓓ   20 Ⓐ Ⓑ Ⓒ Ⓓ   25 Ⓐ Ⓑ Ⓒ Ⓓ

   26 Ⓐ Ⓑ Ⓒ Ⓓ

VERBAL ANALOGIES TEST IV. PART TO WHOLE

1 Ⓐ Ⓑ Ⓒ Ⓓ   6 Ⓐ Ⓑ Ⓒ Ⓓ   11 Ⓐ Ⓑ Ⓒ Ⓓ   16 Ⓐ Ⓑ Ⓒ Ⓓ   21 Ⓐ Ⓑ Ⓒ Ⓓ

2 Ⓐ Ⓑ Ⓒ Ⓓ   7 Ⓐ Ⓑ Ⓒ Ⓓ   12 Ⓐ Ⓑ Ⓒ Ⓓ   17 Ⓐ Ⓑ Ⓒ Ⓓ   22 Ⓐ Ⓑ Ⓒ Ⓓ

3 Ⓐ Ⓑ Ⓒ Ⓓ   8 Ⓐ Ⓑ Ⓒ Ⓓ   13 Ⓐ Ⓑ Ⓒ Ⓓ   18 Ⓐ Ⓑ Ⓒ Ⓓ   23 Ⓐ Ⓑ Ⓒ Ⓓ

4 Ⓐ Ⓑ Ⓒ Ⓓ   9 Ⓐ Ⓑ Ⓒ Ⓓ   14 Ⓐ Ⓑ Ⓒ Ⓓ   19 Ⓐ Ⓑ Ⓒ Ⓓ   24 Ⓐ Ⓑ Ⓒ Ⓓ

5 Ⓐ Ⓑ Ⓒ Ⓓ   10 Ⓐ Ⓑ Ⓒ Ⓓ   15 Ⓐ Ⓑ Ⓒ Ⓓ   20 Ⓐ Ⓑ Ⓒ Ⓓ   25 Ⓐ Ⓑ Ⓒ Ⓓ

   26 Ⓐ Ⓑ Ⓒ Ⓓ

VERBAL ANALOGIES TEST V. PART TO PART

1 Ⓐ Ⓑ Ⓒ Ⓓ	6 Ⓐ Ⓑ Ⓒ Ⓓ	11 Ⓐ Ⓑ Ⓒ Ⓓ	16 Ⓐ Ⓑ Ⓒ Ⓓ	21 Ⓐ Ⓑ Ⓒ Ⓓ
2 Ⓐ Ⓑ Ⓒ Ⓓ	7 Ⓐ Ⓑ Ⓒ Ⓓ	12 Ⓐ Ⓑ Ⓒ Ⓓ	17 Ⓐ Ⓑ Ⓒ Ⓓ	22 Ⓐ Ⓑ Ⓒ Ⓓ
3 Ⓐ Ⓑ Ⓒ Ⓓ	8 Ⓐ Ⓑ Ⓒ Ⓓ	13 Ⓐ Ⓑ Ⓒ Ⓓ	18 Ⓐ Ⓑ Ⓒ Ⓓ	23 Ⓐ Ⓑ Ⓒ Ⓓ
4 Ⓐ Ⓑ Ⓒ Ⓓ	9 Ⓐ Ⓑ Ⓒ Ⓓ	14 Ⓐ Ⓑ Ⓒ Ⓓ	19 Ⓐ Ⓑ Ⓒ Ⓓ	24 Ⓐ Ⓑ Ⓒ Ⓓ
5 Ⓐ Ⓑ Ⓒ Ⓓ	10 Ⓐ Ⓑ Ⓒ Ⓓ	15 Ⓐ Ⓑ Ⓒ Ⓓ	20 Ⓐ Ⓑ Ⓒ Ⓓ	25 Ⓐ Ⓑ Ⓒ Ⓓ
				26 Ⓐ Ⓑ Ⓒ Ⓓ

VERBAL ANALOGIES TEST VI. PURPOSE

1 Ⓐ Ⓑ Ⓒ Ⓓ	6 Ⓐ Ⓑ Ⓒ Ⓓ	11 Ⓐ Ⓑ Ⓒ Ⓓ	16 Ⓐ Ⓑ Ⓒ Ⓓ	21 Ⓐ Ⓑ Ⓒ Ⓓ
2 Ⓐ Ⓑ Ⓒ Ⓓ	7 Ⓐ Ⓑ Ⓒ Ⓓ	12 Ⓐ Ⓑ Ⓒ Ⓓ	17 Ⓐ Ⓑ Ⓒ Ⓓ	22 Ⓐ Ⓑ Ⓒ Ⓓ
3 Ⓐ Ⓑ Ⓒ Ⓓ	8 Ⓐ Ⓑ Ⓒ Ⓓ	13 Ⓐ Ⓑ Ⓒ Ⓓ	18 Ⓐ Ⓑ Ⓒ Ⓓ	23 Ⓐ Ⓑ Ⓒ Ⓓ
4 Ⓐ Ⓑ Ⓒ Ⓓ	9 Ⓐ Ⓑ Ⓒ Ⓓ	14 Ⓐ Ⓑ Ⓒ Ⓓ	19 Ⓐ Ⓑ Ⓒ Ⓓ	24 Ⓐ Ⓑ Ⓒ Ⓓ
5 Ⓐ Ⓑ Ⓒ Ⓓ	10 Ⓐ Ⓑ Ⓒ Ⓓ	15 Ⓐ Ⓑ Ⓒ Ⓓ	20 Ⓐ Ⓑ Ⓒ Ⓓ	25 Ⓐ Ⓑ Ⓒ Ⓓ
				26 Ⓐ Ⓑ Ⓒ Ⓓ

VERBAL ANALOGIES TEST VII. ACTION TO OBJECT

1 Ⓐ Ⓑ Ⓒ Ⓓ	6 Ⓐ Ⓑ Ⓒ Ⓓ	11 Ⓐ Ⓑ Ⓒ Ⓓ	16 Ⓐ Ⓑ Ⓒ Ⓓ	21 Ⓐ Ⓑ Ⓒ Ⓓ
2 Ⓐ Ⓑ Ⓒ Ⓓ	7 Ⓐ Ⓑ Ⓒ Ⓓ	12 Ⓐ Ⓑ Ⓒ Ⓓ	17 Ⓐ Ⓑ Ⓒ Ⓓ	22 Ⓐ Ⓑ Ⓒ Ⓓ
3 Ⓐ Ⓑ Ⓒ Ⓓ	8 Ⓐ Ⓑ Ⓒ Ⓓ	13 Ⓐ Ⓑ Ⓒ Ⓓ	18 Ⓐ Ⓑ Ⓒ Ⓓ	23 Ⓐ Ⓑ Ⓒ Ⓓ
4 Ⓐ Ⓑ Ⓒ Ⓓ	9 Ⓐ Ⓑ Ⓒ Ⓓ	14 Ⓐ Ⓑ Ⓒ Ⓓ	19 Ⓐ Ⓑ Ⓒ Ⓓ	24 Ⓐ Ⓑ Ⓒ Ⓓ
5 Ⓐ Ⓑ Ⓒ Ⓓ	10 Ⓐ Ⓑ Ⓒ Ⓓ	15 Ⓐ Ⓑ Ⓒ Ⓓ	20 Ⓐ Ⓑ Ⓒ Ⓓ	25 Ⓐ Ⓑ Ⓒ Ⓓ
				26 Ⓐ Ⓑ Ⓒ Ⓓ

VERBAL ANALOGIES TEST VIII. OBJECT TO ACTION

1 Ⓐ Ⓑ Ⓒ Ⓓ	6 Ⓐ Ⓑ Ⓒ Ⓓ	11 Ⓐ Ⓑ Ⓒ Ⓓ	16 Ⓐ Ⓑ Ⓒ Ⓓ	21 Ⓐ Ⓑ Ⓒ Ⓓ
2 Ⓐ Ⓑ Ⓒ Ⓓ	7 Ⓐ Ⓑ Ⓒ Ⓓ	12 Ⓐ Ⓑ Ⓒ Ⓓ	17 Ⓐ Ⓑ Ⓒ Ⓓ	22 Ⓐ Ⓑ Ⓒ Ⓓ
3 Ⓐ Ⓑ Ⓒ Ⓓ	8 Ⓐ Ⓑ Ⓒ Ⓓ	13 Ⓐ Ⓑ Ⓒ Ⓓ	18 Ⓐ Ⓑ Ⓒ Ⓓ	23 Ⓐ Ⓑ Ⓒ Ⓓ
4 Ⓐ Ⓑ Ⓒ Ⓓ	9 Ⓐ Ⓑ Ⓒ Ⓓ	14 Ⓐ Ⓑ Ⓒ Ⓓ	19 Ⓐ Ⓑ Ⓒ Ⓓ	24 Ⓐ Ⓑ Ⓒ Ⓓ
5 Ⓐ Ⓑ Ⓒ Ⓓ	10 Ⓐ Ⓑ Ⓒ Ⓓ	15 Ⓐ Ⓑ Ⓒ Ⓓ	20 Ⓐ Ⓑ Ⓒ Ⓓ	25 Ⓐ Ⓑ Ⓒ Ⓓ
				26 Ⓐ Ⓑ Ⓒ Ⓓ

VERBAL ANALOGIES TEXT IX. PLACE

1 Ⓐ Ⓑ Ⓒ Ⓓ	6 Ⓐ Ⓑ Ⓒ Ⓓ	11 Ⓐ Ⓑ Ⓒ Ⓓ	16 Ⓐ Ⓑ Ⓒ Ⓓ	21 Ⓐ Ⓑ Ⓒ Ⓓ
2 Ⓐ Ⓑ Ⓒ Ⓓ	7 Ⓐ Ⓑ Ⓒ Ⓓ	12 Ⓐ Ⓑ Ⓒ Ⓓ	17 Ⓐ Ⓑ Ⓒ Ⓓ	22 Ⓐ Ⓑ Ⓒ Ⓓ
3 Ⓐ Ⓑ Ⓒ Ⓓ	8 Ⓐ Ⓑ Ⓒ Ⓓ	13 Ⓐ Ⓑ Ⓒ Ⓓ	18 Ⓐ Ⓑ Ⓒ Ⓓ	23 Ⓐ Ⓑ Ⓒ Ⓓ
4 Ⓐ Ⓑ Ⓒ Ⓓ	9 Ⓐ Ⓑ Ⓒ Ⓓ	14 Ⓐ Ⓑ Ⓒ Ⓓ	19 Ⓐ Ⓑ Ⓒ Ⓓ	24 Ⓐ Ⓑ Ⓒ Ⓓ
5 Ⓐ Ⓑ Ⓒ Ⓓ	10 Ⓐ Ⓑ Ⓒ Ⓓ	15 Ⓐ Ⓑ Ⓒ Ⓓ	20 Ⓐ Ⓑ Ⓒ Ⓓ	25 Ⓐ Ⓑ Ⓒ Ⓓ
				26 Ⓐ Ⓑ Ⓒ Ⓓ

VERBAL ANALOGIES TEST X. ASSOCIATION

1 Ⓐ Ⓑ Ⓒ Ⓓ	6 Ⓐ Ⓑ Ⓒ Ⓓ	11 Ⓐ Ⓑ Ⓒ Ⓓ	16 Ⓐ Ⓑ Ⓒ Ⓓ	21 Ⓐ Ⓑ Ⓒ Ⓓ
2 Ⓐ Ⓑ Ⓒ Ⓓ	7 Ⓐ Ⓑ Ⓒ Ⓓ	12 Ⓐ Ⓑ Ⓒ Ⓓ	17 Ⓐ Ⓑ Ⓒ Ⓓ	22 Ⓐ Ⓑ Ⓒ Ⓓ
3 Ⓐ Ⓑ Ⓒ Ⓓ	8 Ⓐ Ⓑ Ⓒ Ⓓ	13 Ⓐ Ⓑ Ⓒ Ⓓ	18 Ⓐ Ⓑ Ⓒ Ⓓ	23 Ⓐ Ⓑ Ⓒ Ⓓ
4 Ⓐ Ⓑ Ⓒ Ⓓ	9 Ⓐ Ⓑ Ⓒ Ⓓ	14 Ⓐ Ⓑ Ⓒ Ⓓ	19 Ⓐ Ⓑ Ⓒ Ⓓ	24 Ⓐ Ⓑ Ⓒ Ⓓ
5 Ⓐ Ⓑ Ⓒ Ⓓ	10 Ⓐ Ⓑ Ⓒ Ⓓ	15 Ⓐ Ⓑ Ⓒ Ⓓ	20 Ⓐ Ⓑ Ⓒ Ⓓ	25 Ⓐ Ⓑ Ⓒ Ⓓ
				26 Ⓐ Ⓑ Ⓒ Ⓓ

VERBAL ANALOGIES TEST XI. SEQUENCE

1 Ⓐ Ⓑ Ⓒ Ⓓ	6 Ⓐ Ⓑ Ⓒ Ⓓ	11 Ⓐ Ⓑ Ⓒ Ⓓ	16 Ⓐ Ⓑ Ⓒ Ⓓ	21 Ⓐ Ⓑ Ⓒ Ⓓ
2 Ⓐ Ⓑ Ⓒ Ⓓ	7 Ⓐ Ⓑ Ⓒ Ⓓ	12 Ⓐ Ⓑ Ⓒ Ⓓ	17 Ⓐ Ⓑ Ⓒ Ⓓ	22 Ⓐ Ⓑ Ⓒ Ⓓ
3 Ⓐ Ⓑ Ⓒ Ⓓ	8 Ⓐ Ⓑ Ⓒ Ⓓ	13 Ⓐ Ⓑ Ⓒ Ⓓ	18 Ⓐ Ⓑ Ⓒ Ⓓ	23 Ⓐ Ⓑ Ⓒ Ⓓ
4 Ⓐ Ⓑ Ⓒ Ⓓ	9 Ⓐ Ⓑ Ⓒ Ⓓ	14 Ⓐ Ⓑ Ⓒ Ⓓ	19 Ⓐ Ⓑ Ⓒ Ⓓ	24 Ⓐ Ⓑ Ⓒ Ⓓ
5 Ⓐ Ⓑ Ⓒ Ⓓ	10 Ⓐ Ⓑ Ⓒ Ⓓ	15 Ⓐ Ⓑ Ⓒ Ⓓ	20 Ⓐ Ⓑ Ⓒ Ⓓ	25 Ⓐ Ⓑ Ⓒ Ⓓ
				26 Ⓐ Ⓑ Ⓒ Ⓓ

VERBAL ANALOGIES TEST XII. CHARACTERISTIC

1 Ⓐ Ⓑ Ⓒ Ⓓ	6 Ⓐ Ⓑ Ⓒ Ⓓ	11 Ⓐ Ⓑ Ⓒ Ⓓ	16 Ⓐ Ⓑ Ⓒ Ⓓ	21 Ⓐ Ⓑ Ⓒ Ⓓ
2 Ⓐ Ⓑ Ⓒ Ⓓ	7 Ⓐ Ⓑ Ⓒ Ⓓ	12 Ⓐ Ⓑ Ⓒ Ⓓ	17 Ⓐ Ⓑ Ⓒ Ⓓ	22 Ⓐ Ⓑ Ⓒ Ⓓ
3 Ⓐ Ⓑ Ⓒ Ⓓ	8 Ⓐ Ⓑ Ⓒ Ⓓ	13 Ⓐ Ⓑ Ⓒ Ⓓ	18 Ⓐ Ⓑ Ⓒ Ⓓ	23 Ⓐ Ⓑ Ⓒ Ⓓ
4 Ⓐ Ⓑ Ⓒ Ⓓ	9 Ⓐ Ⓑ Ⓒ Ⓓ	14 Ⓐ Ⓑ Ⓒ Ⓓ	19 Ⓐ Ⓑ Ⓒ Ⓓ	24 Ⓐ Ⓑ Ⓒ Ⓓ
5 Ⓐ Ⓑ Ⓒ Ⓓ	10 Ⓐ Ⓑ Ⓒ Ⓓ	15 Ⓐ Ⓑ Ⓒ Ⓓ	20 Ⓐ Ⓑ Ⓒ Ⓓ	25 Ⓐ Ⓑ Ⓒ Ⓓ
				26 Ⓐ Ⓑ Ⓒ Ⓓ

VERBAL ANALOGIES TEST XIII. DEGREE

1 Ⓐ Ⓑ Ⓒ Ⓓ	6 Ⓐ Ⓑ Ⓒ Ⓓ	11 Ⓐ Ⓑ Ⓒ Ⓓ	16 Ⓐ Ⓑ Ⓒ Ⓓ	21 Ⓐ Ⓑ Ⓒ Ⓓ
2 Ⓐ Ⓑ Ⓒ Ⓓ	7 Ⓐ Ⓑ Ⓒ Ⓓ	12 Ⓐ Ⓑ Ⓒ Ⓓ	17 Ⓐ Ⓑ Ⓒ Ⓓ	22 Ⓐ Ⓑ Ⓒ Ⓓ
3 Ⓐ Ⓑ Ⓒ Ⓓ	8 Ⓐ Ⓑ Ⓒ Ⓓ	13 Ⓐ Ⓑ Ⓒ Ⓓ	18 Ⓐ Ⓑ Ⓒ Ⓓ	23 Ⓐ Ⓑ Ⓒ Ⓓ
4 Ⓐ Ⓑ Ⓒ Ⓓ	9 Ⓐ Ⓑ Ⓒ Ⓓ	14 Ⓐ Ⓑ Ⓒ Ⓓ	19 Ⓐ Ⓑ Ⓒ Ⓓ	24 Ⓐ Ⓑ Ⓒ Ⓓ
5 Ⓐ Ⓑ Ⓒ Ⓓ	10 Ⓐ Ⓑ Ⓒ Ⓓ	15 Ⓐ Ⓑ Ⓒ Ⓓ	20 Ⓐ Ⓑ Ⓒ Ⓓ	25 Ⓐ Ⓑ Ⓒ Ⓓ
				26 Ⓐ Ⓑ Ⓒ Ⓓ

VERBAL ANALOGIES TEST XIV. GRAMMATICAL

1 Ⓐ Ⓑ Ⓒ Ⓓ	6 Ⓐ Ⓑ Ⓒ Ⓓ	11 Ⓐ Ⓑ Ⓒ Ⓓ	16 Ⓐ Ⓑ Ⓒ Ⓓ	21 Ⓐ Ⓑ Ⓒ Ⓓ
2 Ⓐ Ⓑ Ⓒ Ⓓ	7 Ⓐ Ⓑ Ⓒ Ⓓ	12 Ⓐ Ⓑ Ⓒ Ⓓ	17 Ⓐ Ⓑ Ⓒ Ⓓ	22 Ⓐ Ⓑ Ⓒ Ⓓ
3 Ⓐ Ⓑ Ⓒ Ⓓ	8 Ⓐ Ⓑ Ⓒ Ⓓ	13 Ⓐ Ⓑ Ⓒ Ⓓ	18 Ⓐ Ⓑ Ⓒ Ⓓ	23 Ⓐ Ⓑ Ⓒ Ⓓ
4 Ⓐ Ⓑ Ⓒ Ⓓ	9 Ⓐ Ⓑ Ⓒ Ⓓ	14 Ⓐ Ⓑ Ⓒ Ⓓ	19 Ⓐ Ⓑ Ⓒ Ⓓ	24 Ⓐ Ⓑ Ⓒ Ⓓ
5 Ⓐ Ⓑ Ⓒ Ⓓ	10 Ⓐ Ⓑ Ⓒ Ⓓ	15 Ⓐ Ⓑ Ⓒ Ⓓ	20 Ⓐ Ⓑ Ⓒ Ⓓ	25 Ⓐ Ⓑ Ⓒ Ⓓ
				26 Ⓐ Ⓑ Ⓒ Ⓓ